Pacific Ocean
Timor Sea
Torres Strait
Arnhem Land
Kakadu
Cape York
Peninsula
Coral Sea
Kimberley Ranges
The Great
Barrier Reef
Daintree
The Pilbara
Wet
Tropics
Uluru
Great
Artesian
Basin
Fraser Island
Central Desert Region
The
Great
Dividing
Range
The Nullarbor
Lake
Eyre
Norfolk Island
Lord Howe Island
Murray-
Darling Basin
erance
The Great
Australian Bight
The Blue
Mountains
The
Mallee
Kangaroo Island
Gippsland
Tasman Sea
King Island
Bass Strait
Tasmania
Port of Hobart
Southern Ocean
New Zealand
Macquarie Island

Australia's

Endangered BUSH CREATURES

Myke Mollard

For Annabelle

Carnaby's Black-Cockatoos

Squawking their way across the Western Australian wheatbelt are our majestic Carnaby's Black-Cockatoos.

Due to a 50% decline in their population over the past 50 years, our **Carnaby's** are now considered endangered. If we aren't careful this sunset hallabaloo may soon become a rare sight.

Woodslane Press

Australia's Endangered Bush Creatures

**We share this earth with many creatures great and small.
They have evolved over hundreds of thousands to millions of years to live in balance with and help sustain their environments - the same environments that define and enable our very existence. This is the story of the most endangered of these creatures, a passionate story that has shaped my affinity for nature and wildlife. Whether because of mankind's destructive footprint or brutal natural disasters, some of these creatures are being pushed to the brink of extinction. Their survival is a measure of the likelihood of our survival, for we are all earthlings and share this planet with these precious creatures. We are part of this land, just passing through this timeless, sunburnt country. "Mother Earth" provides me with the grandeur, beauty, diversity and wonderment with which to illustrate my books, but these are also a consistent reminder of how important it is to protect as much of Earth's diversity of life as possible.**

The Plight of our Parrots

Australia has often been described as "The land of the Parrots". With 56 species of wild parrots out of 300 known worldwide, we truly hold a treasure trove of these colourful birds. Sadly, a third of all parrots are on the brink of extinction and Australia is haunted by the tragic unnecessary loss of the Paradise Parrot within this century.

The **Paradise Parrot** story is an important case for wildlife conservation. It maybe "our only parrot extinction" on record, but it's a timely reminder of how colonisation has devastated our fragile balance of nature. Australia hosts a variety of parrots; cockatoos, lorikeets, rosellas, budgerigars and ringnecks, with only five species found elsewhere in the world. This highlights how important ongoing efforts in conservation are for these wonderful bush creatures.

Of these parrots, several are endangered. One is the fast, agile and very aptly named **Swift Parrot**. It breeds in Tasmania during the summer months and migrates north to the south eastern mainland between Brisbane and Melbourne and west as far as Adelaide. Their range, migratory patterns and their unique diet and nesting choices have put this gorgeous parrot on the Endangered watchlist.

Likewise, the limited range and elusive nature of the the **Western Ground Parrot**, very similar to the **Eastern Ground Parrot** in appearance, has raised grave concerns in recent years as little is known about the health of these fragile western parrot populations.

Which brings us to the Australian **Night Parrot**, the most elusive of them all. First recorded in 1845, the last living specimen was collected in 1912. Until the next sighting in 1979 it was thought to be extinct. In 2013 naturalist John Young captured several photos of a live bird in Queensland.

The story of the **Paradise Parrot** and these three endangered parrots highlights how critically needed the Endangered species list is, and how it helps with efforts to preserve endangered creatures from our environmental impacts.

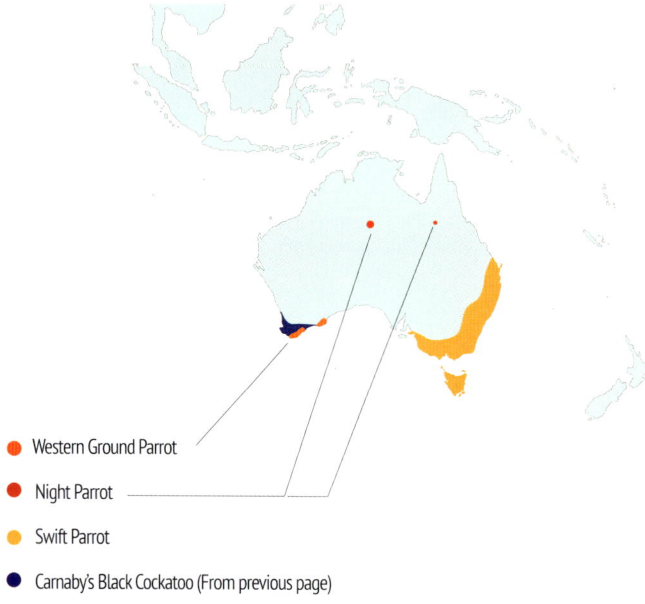

THIS PAGE
Top; Two strikingly beautiful Swift Parrots are perched in the scrub, a few are in the distance flying swiftly by.

Middle; a pair of rarely seen and shy Western Ground Parrots.

Bottom; The most elusive of all Australian parrots, the mysterious Night Parrot.

THIS PAGE
The Orange-bellied Parrot nesting in south-west Tasmania.

OPPOSITE PAGE
The Yellow Chat "Capricorn" Subspecies (Female Left) and "Alligator River" Subspecies (Male in flight).

Orange-bellied Parrot

The amazing orange-bellied parrot is one of only three species of parrot that migrates. This small "grass parrot" breeds in eucalypt hollows, bordering button grass moors, in south-west Tasmania and spends the winter on the marshland coast of southern mainland Australia near Queenscliff, Victoria.

The **Orange-bellied Parrot**, as its name suggests, has an orange patch on its belly. Their unique migration and very specialised choice of terrain have made them extremely susceptible to human impacts on their natural habitat: feral cats and foxes, the spread of introduced weeds, habitat loss and now genetic factors due to inbreeding have greatly impacted their population. The **Orange-bellied Parrot** is another of Australia's most Critically Endangered bird species, with less than 50 parrots making up the wild population.

In 2017 the known population dwindled to 14. If it wasn't for well managed conservation and captive breeding programmes, this amazing little grass parrot may have gone extinct on our watch.

Appearance *Bright green head, neck and upper parts. Yellow-green to Lime green breast, abdomen and flanks, with an orange belly. Also a distinctive, two-toned blue frontal band.* **Size** *Approximately 20cm long from beak to tail tip.*

Yellow Chats

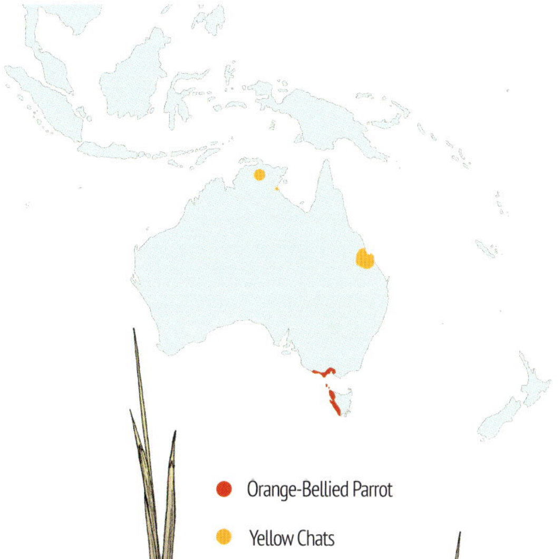

Not all Yellow Chats are considered Critically Endangered. Yet both the "Capricorn" and "Alligator River" subspecies of Yellow Chat are.

The **Yellow Chat** is a small bird that forages on the ground in dense scrub grass, saltbush and low shrubs. Insectivorous, they scavenge for food in these pockets of damp vegetation on the arid coast, near shallow waterholes and ponds. Feral pigs, water buffalo and cattle trample important breeding habitats for these birds.

Appearance *Bright golden-yellow forehead and underparts, males have a black crescent breast band. Their crown and neck can be a grey-olive colour, their back is yellow-brown and tail black with yellow tips.*
Size *Approximately 11cm tall.*

Endangered Scrubland Birds

Once common throughout savannah country, scrub plains and woodlands across Australia, several bird species have declined dramatically in the past few decades and now live in very restricted areas. In the Northern Territory, the famous, brightly-coloured Gouldian Finch (named after Elizabeth Gould the artist, but also sometimes known as the Rainbow or Painted Finch) is diminishing alarmingly in the wild. The Plains Wanderer, Spotted Quail-Thrust and Thick-billed Grasswren are also disappearing. Today just a few small and scattered populations across south-eastern Australia remain. Their stories of highly specialised lifestyles combined with specific environments are not unique. On King Island, in Bass Strait, the King Island Scrub-tit has reached the brink of extinction. At the last review, its isolated population in Nook Swamps was down to only 20 birds. Little other than rarity is known about them and unless more is done they could soon be gone forever.

Across Australia, the cause of a lot of our birds' habitat destruction is grazing by feral animals, mostly horses, deer, goats and pigs. Farming, land clearing for crops and invasive weeds contribute significantly to the impact. Resulting changes in overall vegetation can isolate populations into small, separated and vulnerable pockets if left unchecked. The widespread change from traditional burning by indigenous custodians to modern inappropriate fire regimes is another dangerous development: it has been pinpointed as the cause of the extinction of the **Paradise Parrot** at Darling Downs. The disruption of traditional cycles of fire, drought and rain is thought to have impacted many of our savannah, plains, desert and scrubland birds. A balanced and self-regulating habitat is so important: an out of balance ecosystem creates unnecessary competition for resources, which can weaken individuals of many of the member species, promoting conditions for hardship and disease.

Added to this, the **Gouldian Finch** is also threatened by over-harvesting by unlicensed bird trappers and illegal poaching from the exotic bird and petshop trade. Like Australian parrots, their striking colours and character are prized and desired around the world.

In the story of climate change, endangered species such as the **Gouldian Finch**, **Plains Wanderer**, **Spotted Quail-Thrush** and **Thick-billed Grasswren** are the canaries in the mine shaft, warning miners of pending doom. Their complexity and diversity, and their wide ranges of behaviours and adaptions to our often harsh Australian environments are sometimes no proof against rapidly changing conditions. All species are links in a chain and help nature sustain an ecological balance - remove the links and the balance can soon be tipped into a far less sustainable mode.

It's worth reflecting that if we didn't discover a small isolated population like the **King Island Scrub-tit**, we might not know they even existed. It's estimated that hundreds of creatures around the world are disappearing before we even discover them. Surprisingly little is known about the natural world and the advantages each species offers to its ecosystem.

OPPOSITE PAGE

Top; Three Gouldian Finches, one with a black-face morph, while the other two have crimson colours.

Top right; a Plains Wanderer stands tall, striding through the wildflower plains of the Riverina.

Middle; a Spotted Quail-thrush struts his stuff while two Quail-Thrush chicks hide in the undergrowth to his left.

Bottom; two smooth, faun-coloured King Island Scrub-tits (left), their eyes grey-white rimmed; hopping through the shrubs to their right are two dappled brown/white Thick-billed Grasswrens.

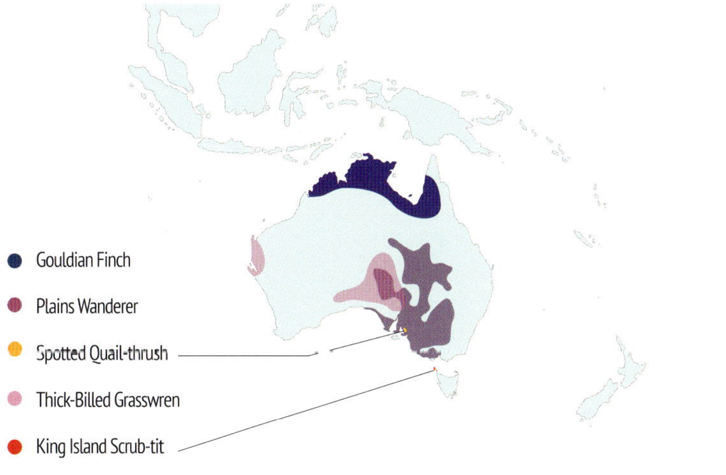

Helmeted Honeyeater

Victoria's State emblem is the sweetest little honeyeater! When you discover their tiny pocket of forest near Yellingbo Conservation Reserve you will understand the importance of the effort that has been made to save this critically endangered species from extinction.

These little Honeyeaters are the largest of four known **Tufted Honeyeaters**. They can be easily identified by their distinctive yellow tufts on either side of their heads. If you are lucky, you may have encounted these birds and the efforts of the Melbourne Zoo and Healesville Sanctuary to bring this species back from the brink of extinction.

A decade ago, the estimate of our total wild **Helmeted Honeyeater** population dropped to just 50 birds. With an extremely limited range, and needing a streamside swamp forest to breed and thrive, conservation efforts have been established to reintroduce semi-wild populations in the forests east of Melbourne. Still with fewer than 250 birds in the wild, the three remaining populations are growing, but there are the constant threats of bushfires, feral cats, foxes and the changing climate that could still see this creature disappear completely.

Appearance *They are black, yellow and olive-brown in colour with a bright yellow crest or helmet which distinguishes them from all other honeyeaters.* **Size** *Approximately 20cm from bill to tail tip.*

Regent Honeyeater

Historical speaking, the Regent Honeyeater was once a very common bird. In fact, around the early 1900s "Regents" were seen as our most common honeyeater within its range, which extended from South Australia, across Victoria, New South Wales all the way to Rockhampton in Queensland.

Thriving in flowering forests and open woodland areas that contain good nectar and nesting resources, such as box gums and ironbarks, the **Regent Honeyeater** has seen its population plummet in recent years to fewer than 350 birds. It is now completely extinct in South Australia, and rare in Victoria and Queensland, where habitat has contracted severely. There are now three major breeding sites - in Bundarra-Barraba, Capertee Valley and another in the north-east of Victoria – and all three were devastated by the 2020 bushfires. **Regents** are now one of Australia's most critically endangered species and the race is on to preserve and save this bird from extinction in the wild.

Appearance *The Regent Honeyeater is a striking and distinctive, medium-sized, black and yellow honeyeater with a sturdy, curved bill.* **Size** *Approximately 20-24cm long with a wing-span of 30cm*

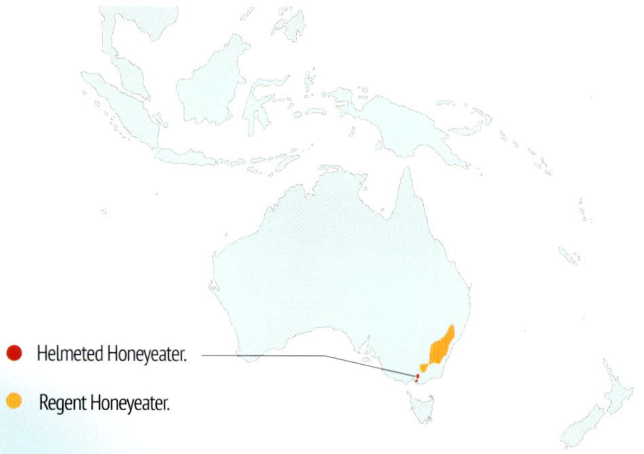

OPPOSITE PAGE
The Regent Honeyeater perched on a limb of a flowering gum.

THIS PAGE
Helmeted Honeyeaters feeding in breeding season.

Southern Greater Sooty Owl

Rarely seen, relatively little is known about the Greater Sooty Owl and its conservation status wavers between Vulnerable and Endangered. In the central highlands of Victoria there is a logging threat to the owl's Mountain Ash strongholds. On the other side of the great dividing range, the catastrophic 2020 bushfires across New South Wales and Victoria saw millions of hectares of prime Sooty Owl hunting grounds go up in smoke. These elusive owls and their environment need protection and time to recover.

Most of us are familiar with the Barn Owl. Sleek white creatures dappled with dark brown spots, ripples and flecks of tan and light brown feathers. But Australia has eleven Owl species. The **Southern Greater Sooty Owl** of the mountain Ash forests of Victoria's central highlands is the most endangered. These silent nocturnal hunters, prey on Sugar gliders and ringtail possums. But they also hunt a wide range of native animals including the greater glider, bandicoots, rodents and smaller native antechinuses. They will even snack on small birds, bats, large moths and insects. These gorgeous owls are sedentary and territorial, living out their lives in one area or range. Walking a bush-track at night through these giant mountain ash strongholds, you might be lucky to hear their piercing shriek by the light of a full moon. It's a whistling call that can last up to two seconds and resembles the sound of a falling bomb.

Most of us will never see these majestic night creatures in the wild. They keep to themselves, roosting in large tree hollows, caves or in dense foliage during daylight. These owls prefer roosting and nesting in deep gullies in moist eucalyptus forests, with smooth-barked gum trees, tree ferns and a wet forest understory full of lilly pilly and dense shrubs. They may hunt in drier areas, but usually roost and breed in the moister, darker recesses of our great southern forests.

Such is the elusiveness of the **Greater Sooty Owl** that the total population has not yet been reliably quantified. Populations have been discovered up the eastern coast of Australia as far as Queensland and some have been seen on Flinders Island in the Bass Strait. While these owls often hunt and live alongside Australia's largest owl, the **Powerful Owl**, and compete with them for food, the main threat to this owl's existence is that of logging for grazing, agriculture, forestry or other development.

Bushfires are also a threat and regular preventative burning effects the quality of ground cover for mammals and other prey, particularly in drier more open forests.

In New South Wales and Victoria the **Greater Sooty Owl** is protected, so any loss of appropriate mature hollow-bearing trees or dramatic changes to the woodland structure is now (in theory) prevented. However, past clearing of forest habitat for grazing, agriculture, forestry and other developments has already impacted these owls significantly. A more recent danger to a variety of owl species has been, surprisingly, the recent mice plague - because of the secondary poisoning from rodenticides.

Appearance *The owl has a dark grey "sooty black" facial disk. They have a finely white-spotted head with scattered white spots on their back and wings. Their upper body feathers are dark gray or sooty black and get darker as they age. The underside is lighter. Their legs are feathered, and they have a short tail. The females appear to be larger and lighter in colour than the males.* **Size** *They grow to around 36-43cm in length and have a wingspan of around 80cm.*

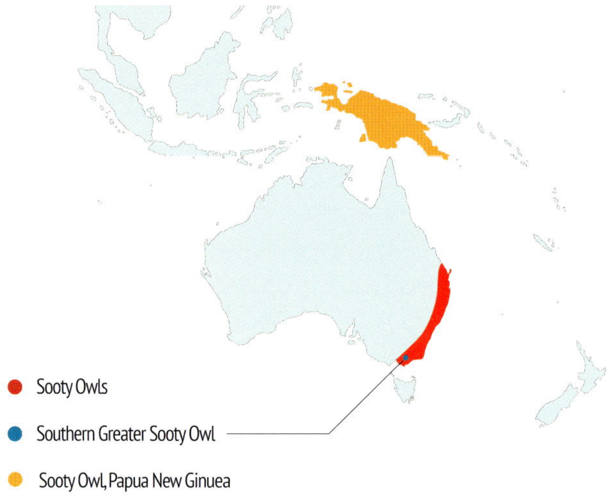

OPPOSITE PAGE
If logging of our old growth forests is stopped, there is real hope for these two breeding Greater Sooty Owls.

The Frigatebird and Petrels

Australia is blessed with 8,222 islands surrounding the mainland. A land girt by sea! The islands within the Tasman Sea, Torres Strait, parts of the Indian Ocean and extending as far as the Pacific Ocean are used by many sea-fairing birds. They breed on oceanic islands, sandy atolls, even boulders of rock jutting out of the sea, nesting on cliff ledges, ridges or rocky slopes. Unfortunately some islands are now plagued by feral cats and rats.

The **Christmas Island Frigatebird** is a distinctive but now endangered bird. Ranging over both Australian and Indonesian waters, Christmas Island is the only place in the world where it breeds, nesting in the forest canopy. The male has a bright red throat pouch, called a 'gular', that it blows up like a fancy balloon. These **Frigatebirds** primarily forage in the ocean for food, scooping up marine organisms such as fish and squid. Over-fishing effects food availability, which has contributed to the decline of these seabirds, while the spread of feral cats and yellow crazy ants is also curtailing nesting opportunities on the island.

While these **Frigatebirds** might be the most colourful seabirds to be on Australia's endangered list, this isn't a popularity contest. There are actually three mysterious **Petrels** that grace our islands and shores. A few of these seabirds are so elusive that not much is known about them. The **Herald Petrel** is a lightly built petrel of offshore tropical waters, known across the Pacific but not seen from mainland Australia. Its plumage is highly variable, from white-body and dark-head to mostly dark. It has dark wings with white-cream flashes on the underside. They visit colonies in daytime to feed, and pairs chase around high overhead.

The second petrel is **Beck's Petrel**, mostly dark-brown with a white underbody and a strongly hooded appearance. It has a small, thin bill, more rounded wings and an apparently 'erratic' flying style. **Beck's Petrel** was first described in 1928, seen again in 1929 then disappeared until the early 2000s when the Petrels were confirmed to still exist. They are now considered critically endangered. In 2010 a **Beck's Petrel** landed on a chartered birdwatching cruise ship in the Tasman Sea, and was briefly studied before being released.

The third petrel is the **Round Island Petrel** or **Trindade Petrel**. This petrel has a few color morphs: dark and light, as well as some in-between morphs. Theses little known Pacific birds were determined to be distinct from the **Herald Petrel**, and as they do use Round Island they were aptly named. They nest on cliff ledges, ridges or rocky slopes on remote islands, but again rats have found their way to some of these islands from ships. Egg predation causes stress and habitat loss. With small breeding ranges to begin with, all these Petrel species are now listed as endangered.

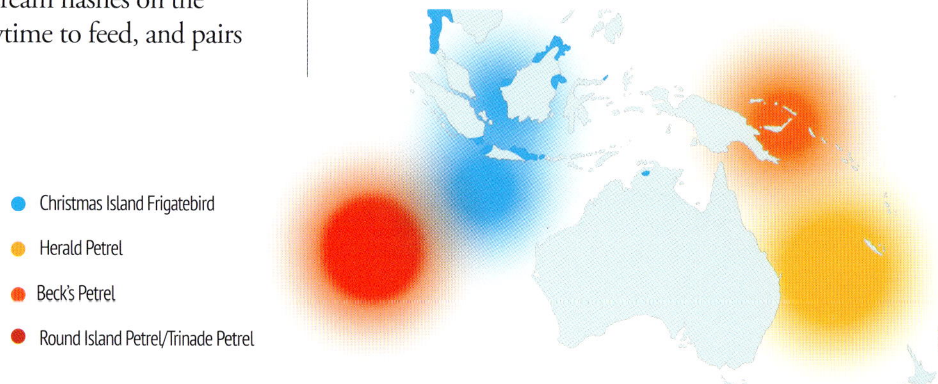

THIS PAGE
Top Left; Two Herald Petrels hunt out on the high seas.
Top Right; Three Beck's Petrels hunt for a feed.
Bottom; Round Island Petrel or Trunidade Petrel soars over the storm swell.

OPPOSITE PAGE
Christmas Island Frigatebirds nest while a young male soars amongst the tall island palms.

THIS PAGE

Top left; five Curlew Sandpipers hunt in the mangroves at low tide.

Top right; two Great Knots forage after a long migration from the other side of the world.

Below left; three Bar-tailed Godwits take off from the coastal estuary.

Bottom right; two Eastern Curlews in the evening light.

The Great Migrating Sandpipers

Australia's wetland birds are remarkably diverse. Some wetland birds remain on the wetlands, lakes, mangroves, coastal beachs, inland waterways and estuarine tidal ecosystems all year round, while others migrate across avian-skyways to the four corners of the earth, some as far as Russia, China, Alaska or the Arctic Circle. This is the story of our critically endangered migrating shorebirds.

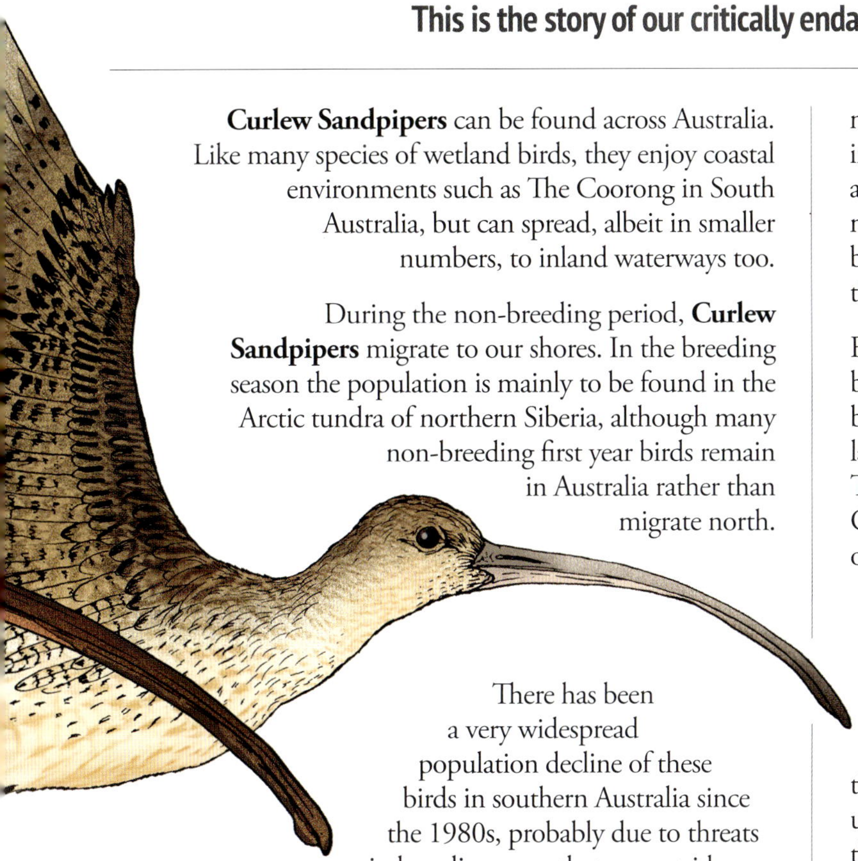

Curlew Sandpipers can be found across Australia. Like many species of wetland birds, they enjoy coastal environments such as The Coorong in South Australia, but can spread, albeit in smaller numbers, to inland waterways too.

During the non-breeding period, **Curlew Sandpipers** migrate to our shores. In the breeding season the population is mainly to be found in the Arctic tundra of northern Siberia, although many non-breeding first year birds remain in Australia rather than migrate north.

There has been a very widespread population decline of these birds in southern Australia since the 1980s, probably due to threats in breeding areas that are outside Australia. But while these seasonal visitors wait out their winter in our intertidal habitats, our human disturbance at roost and feeding sites, threats from dogs on beaches, as well as pollution are the most likely causes for their dramatic population collapse.

Another Sandpiper that visits our shores is the **Great Knot**, a medium-sized shorebird which also breeds in the Arctic circle in the far north of Canada, Europe, and Russia. Their diet varies depending on the season: arthropods, insect larvae are preferred in the breeding season, while various small crustaceans and hard-shelled molluscs are consumed on mudflats during their winter stay. While worldwide the population decline is slight or of limited concern, many local declines have been noted here in Australia.

Bar-tailed Godwits, again from the Sandpiper family, hold the world distance record for their non-stop flight between Alaska to New Zealand. Recorded as flying 11,000km in 8 days, the birds lose almost 50% of their body weight along the way. Arriving in Australia, to our rich and abundant mudflats, fully stocked with tasty treats, they fatten back up in no time. Females are bigger than males and overall these are quite large waders. The **Bar-tailed Godwit** is mainly mottled brown above and lighter, more buff below. The breeding plumage is darker, more rufous, with females duller than males and young birds resembling non-breeding birds.

Finally, the **Eastern Curlew** is a large wader, mostly flecked brown and buff all over. They have a very long down-curved black bill which is pink at the base. This is not only the largest curlew, but probably the world's largest sandpiper. The Eastern Curlew breeds in Russia and north-eastern China, but its distribution is poorly known. Over the course of a year, an **Eastern Curlew** will fly more than 20,000km migrating to and fro. By the end of its migration it has lost up to 70% of its body weight and its muscles have begun to be digested for energy.

Human disturbance has been identified as one of the major threats to all these shorebirds. Our impacts reduce the amount of resting time the birds have, forcing them to use excessive energy at a time when they need to conserve their reserves for the next migration. It's believed that if the birds don't get enough food and rest, they either fail to get to the breeding grounds at all or arrive with a reduced ability to breed at the end of their flight.

Endangered Frogs are Disappearing

In the beautiful rainforests of North Queensland, the cool, shady micro-climates of the understory of the wet tropics hold amazing diversity. Upland streams and creeks cascade over rocks, producing fast-flowing torrents and mossy homes for a host of frog species. Yet in recent years these once abundant populations have mysteriously collapsed. The primary cause of this is most likely the chytrid fungus, which has affected most amphibians globally.

The **Sharp-snouted Day Frog**, or **Sharp-nosed Torrent Frog**, is endemic to upland rainforest streams of north-eastern Queensland. Active during the day and once locally abundant in these remote untouched areas, its population decline started around 1988. Despite them being listed as critically endangered, efforts to monitor and assist failed to help. The last sighting was in 1997 and it is very likely to soon be presumed extinct.

Tucked away on Thornton Peak is another small frog called The **Elegant Frog** or **Beautiful Nursery Frog**. As with any small range, threats such as as tourist development and global warming can - and have - disturbed its world significantly. It's only a small species, reaching up to nearly 3cm in length. It has a grey or brown back, with or without orange or red patches. The belly is white, with red and orange patches and also black specks. Fingers and toes are unwebbed, with larger finger and toe discs.

A world away, in Western Australian, a commonly known species of frog, the **White-bellied Frog**, hides out in swampland near Margaret River. A small frog, it occupies crevices and mossy, swampy depressions adjoining small creeks. Threats from altered ecology have turned this frog's world upside down.

Threats such as fire, disease, the spread of weeds and livestock trampling can degrade river bank vegetation surrounding the frog's habitat. Introduced tree species can also alter the local hydrology and water temperature. Now critically endangered, efforts are being made to stabilise this frog's populations. The local community and rangers are working to ensure its survival, with plans in Forest Grove and Blackwood River National Parks to assist the protection of the frog's habitat.

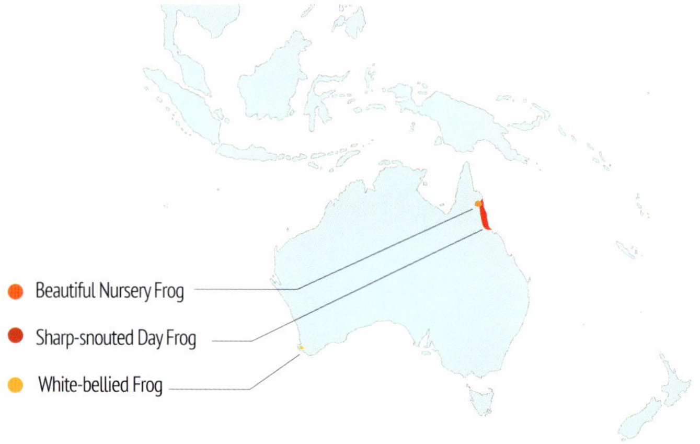

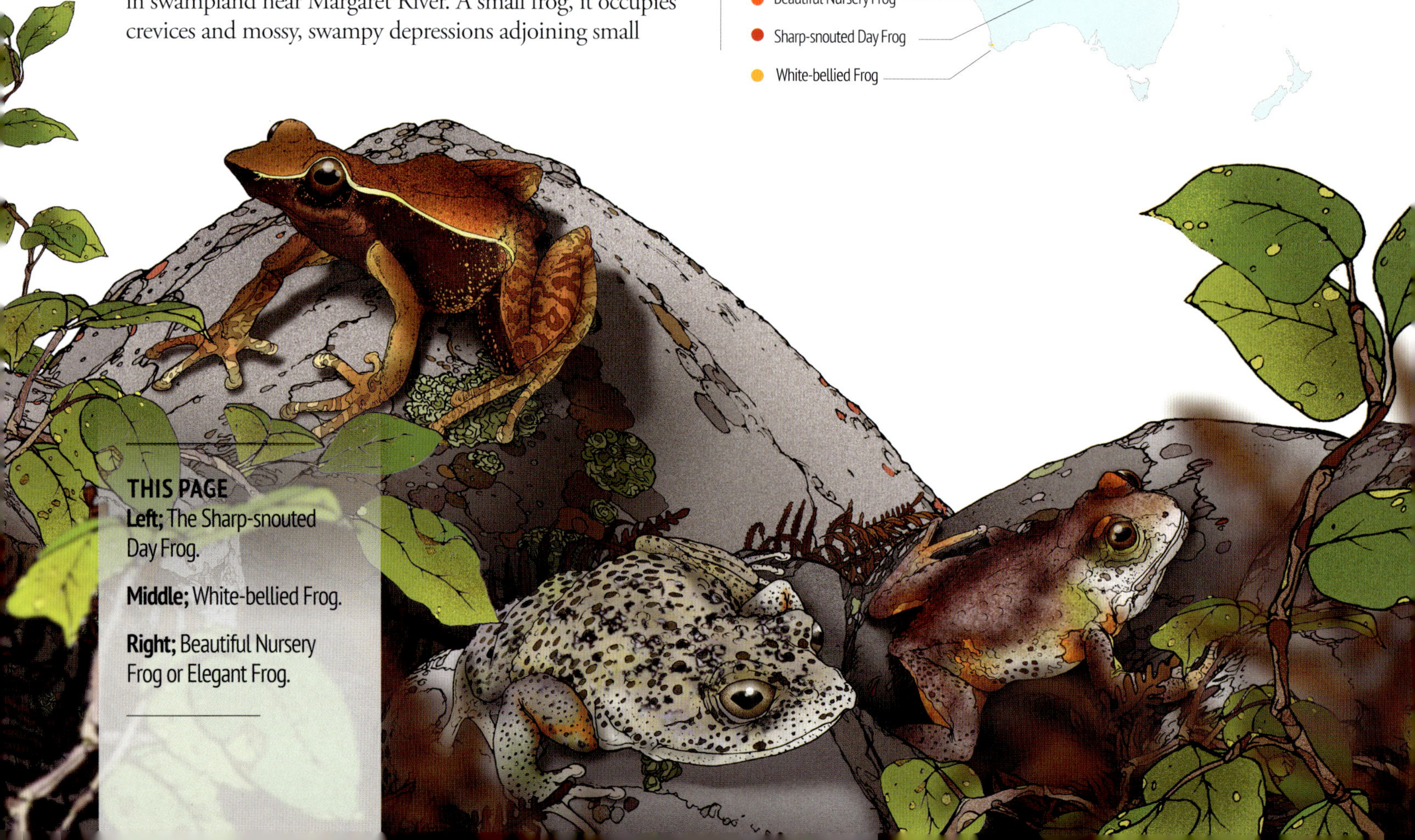

THIS PAGE
Left; The Sharp-snouted Day Frog.

Middle; White-bellied Frog.

Right; Beautiful Nursery Frog or Elegant Frog.

Our Precious Tree Frogs, Out on a Limb!

From the New England Tablelands in New South Wales, to the moist lowland forest of subtropical Queensland, the frogs are calling. In the wild, it's often hard to see these tiny bush creatures, but seasonally you can hear the calls, croaks and chorus of our tuneful tree frogs.

The **Yellow-spotted Tree Frog** (also know as the **New England Swamp Frog**, **Tablelands Bell Frog** or **Yellow-spotted Bell Frog**) is one of our critically endangered frogs. It is found in the New England tableland region, living near in trees along rivers, next to temperate grasslands, swamps, freshwater lakes, marshes and shallow ponds common to the area.

By 1980 this tree frog had all but disappeared and was believed to be extinct. However, in late 2009 a surviving wild population was located and a small, highly protected "insurance" colony was established in a new location - and not a moment too soon as the original wild colony was wiped out by severe flooding and the chytrid fungus disease.

Also endemic to a small isolated area of the northern tablelands of New South Wales, the **Peppered Tree Frog** is known from only five stream systems in the wild. After searches in these streams and adjacent areas, this species has not been located in the wild since the 1970s. A similar story to the **Yellow-spotted Frog**, except that we are still hoping to find a surviving wild population.

In the subtropical wilds of these moist lowland forests, close to streams and rivers, **Spencer's River Tree Frog** or **Spencer's Tree frog**, more commonly referred to as the **Spotted Tree Frog** used to thrive in great numbers. Today it's seen a decline due to severe habitat loss and human impact.

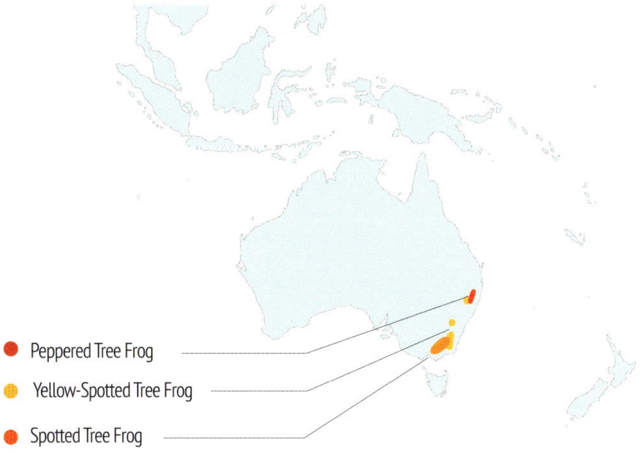

THIS PAGE

Top left; The Yellow-spotted Tree Frog.

Top right; Spencer's Tree Frog or Spotted Tree Frog.

Bottom; The Peppered Tree Frog.

Mission Critical for the Baw Baw Frog

Most Australians have no idea about this small forest dwelling amphibian called the Baw Baw Frog. Wild populations are estimated to have declined by more than 98% since the 1980s. Crippled by a disease, caused by the Amphibian Chytrid Fungus, extinction was likely in just five to ten years.

Frogs are a critical indicator, helping us assess the health of our forest and watershed environments. Population fluctuations are a normal part of nature, but violent crashes are rare and may indicate stresses on the ecological health of an environment. In such a situation, if left unchecked, diseases such as viruses and fungi can decimate isolated communities and easily produce a population collapse in under a decade. It looks like we have anticipated and hopefully stopped the **Baw Baw Frog** extinction event in time. Thanks to Australian zoos and their "fighting extinction" programme, a captive breeding initiative has so far ensured the **Baw Baw Frog's** survival. The programme, begun in 2010, saw the first eggs laid in captivity in 2018 and by November 2020 it was estimated that about 1,000 of these frogs now live in the wild.

Appearance *The frogs have a prominent gland behind each eye. Adults are dark brown, with textured lumpy skin. Can be mottled light and dark brown, with yellow flecked bellies.* **Size** *Adult length is between is 42-55mm.*

Mysterious Mistfrogs

The **Mountain Mistfrog** and **Armoured Mistfrog** are both localised species in the wet tropics, once abundant amongst the fast moving upland streams, waterfalls and cascades of northeastern Queensland. In the late 1980s and early 1990s their populations suffered dramatic declines and they have all but disappeared, despite being well adapted to life in the upper rainforests.

The **Armoured Mistfrog** lives only near the splash zones of waterfalls, sticking to the rocks and jumping away to safety when disturbed. The primary reason usually sited for their decline is the amphibian chytrid fungus, which has affected many amphibians globally.

Both species appeared to have gone extinct, but recent surveys and expeditions have discovered hopeful evidence of previously unknown colonies. There are also two other species, the **Waterfall Mistfrog** and **Common Mistfrog**, that could also follow suit.

The fates of the Mountain Mistfrog and Armoured Mistfrog are unknown. Their habitat has been protected since 1988, therefore habitat destruction is no longer a threat.

THIS PAGE
Two Baw Baw Frogs tangled in a range of damp mosses in an old growth southern rainforest.

OPPOSITE PAGE
Left; The Mountain Mistfrog and **right;** the dappled Armoured Mistfrog.

A Range of Rare Frogs

From the the North Tablelands of New South Wales to the humid mountains on the coast of south-east Queensland, a number of little frogs living in small fast-flowing streams are, sadly, critically endangered.

THIS PAGE
Above left; Northern Tinker Frog.
Abover middle; Two Eungella Torrent Frogs.
Above right; Two Kroombit Tinker Frogs.
Front left; Booroolong Frog on mossy log.

The **Booroolong Frog** is a species of stream-dwelling frog native to the Great Dividing Range in New South Wales. This frog reaches about 45mm in length. It is normally brown with pale spots or mottling, slightly warty in appearance, and the flanks are grey. This species was once abundant in streams, until drastic declines began to occur in the Northern Tablelands where it is now only found in two streams near Tamworth. The introduction of fish such as trout, plus the ever-threatening chytrid fungus are believed to be the main causes for decline.

The rare **Eungella Torrent Frog** is restricted to the ranges west of Mackay in Queensland, from Clarke Range in the north to Finch Hatton Gorge in the south, at altitudes between 200-1,000 metres. It was considered common across these ranges until January 1985, when the first signs of the decline were observed at lower altitudes. A small population was recorded in June 1986 but disappeared until May 1987. After another period of apparent absence, a lone individual was discovered in 1992 and the species has since been recorded within Eungella National Park. Forest grazing and trampling of stream-side vegetation by livestock may have been factors in its decline. The spread of cane toads is another possible cause. There isn't enough research to firmly blame either at this stage.

The **Kroombit Tinker Frog**, also sometimes referred to as **Pleione's Torrent Frog**, is endemic to Central Queensland. It lives among rocks and leaf litter near small flowing streams and not much is known about this rare species.

Similariy, the **Northern Tinker Frog** or **Tinkling frog** is from the same the family and endemic to more humid mountainous areas of north-eastern Queensland. Queensland is a hotspot for many of our rare frog species and this rarely studied nocturnal frog lives among rocks and logs in small fast-flowing streams. Both of these species appear to be threatened with extinction.

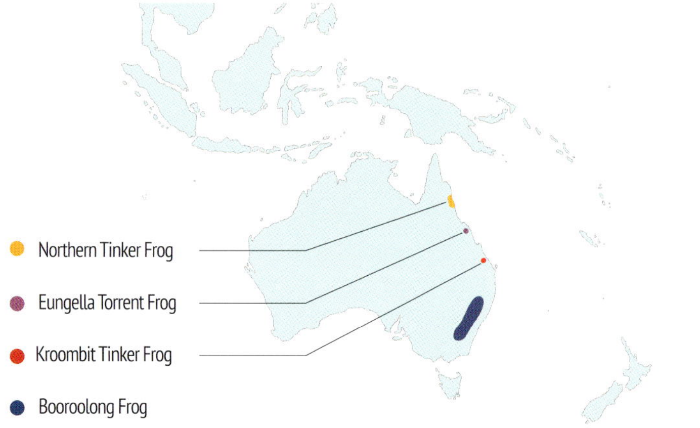

The Visually Striking Corroboree Frogs

One of Australia's tiny little treasures, the Corroboree frog is only found in the sub-alpine regions of the Australian Capital Territory and the Mount Kosciuszko National Park. It hibernates during the winter under fallen snow gum leaves or curls of bark and in spring hunts in the moist alpine moss.

The two species of ground dwelling **Corroboree Frog** are both poisonous and were the first vertebrates discovered that produce their own poison without getting it through their diet, as many other frogs do. The **Southern Corroboree** is recognised as Critically Endangered, while the **Northern Corroboree** is listed as Endangered. The causes are principally habitat destruction by 4-wheel driving, ski resort development and introduced feral animals like pigs, deer and brumby herds. Research and captive breeding is underway to save these precious frogs from extinction.

Appearance *The Southern Corroboree Frog is a visually stunning frog, bi-coloured Yellow and Black with sometimes pale yellow-green or white spots on its toes and underbelly. The Northern Corroboree Frog form looks blacker having slightly narrower longitudinal yellow stripes, but doesn't grow as large as the Southern morph.*
Size *They're tiny! Only growing to around 2.5-3cm.*

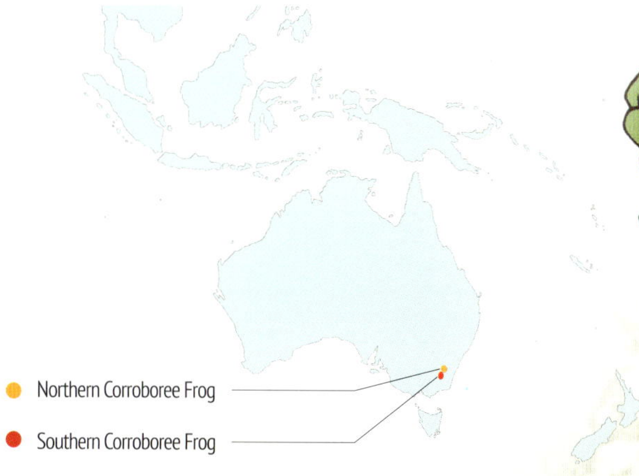

THIS PAGE
Left; two Northern Corroboree frogs.

Right; two Southern Corroboree frogs.

The Ornate Hawksbill Sea Turtle

The critically endangered Hawksbill Sea Turtle travels the oceans of the world, living a part of its life in the open oceans. However, it spends most of its time in the sanctuary of warm shallow lagoons and reefs such as the Great Barrier Reef. Hunted for their decorative shells, critical declines have also come about through human 'by-catch' fishing practices, pollution in our oceans and the faltering health of reef ecosystems brought on by climate change.

In the past century, there's been an estimated eighty percent loss of the **Hawksbill Sea Turtle** population. This decline is likely caused by a combination of climate change and the fact that humans have killed many adult turtles (through accident and deliberately - they were prized for their shells). Their slow growth and reproductive rates inhibit population recovery.

Their existence is also under threat from ocean pollution and the loss of nesting areas because of expanding coastal developments worldwide. **Hawksbills** evidently reach maturity after 20 years and are genetically distinct from other turtles. Thus, as a unique and endangered species, they will be a real focus for conservation efforts in the future.

Little else is known about these creatures. What is known is that, due to their diet of venomous cnidarians, their meat is toxic. They are the only primarily spongivorous reptile and they were the first reptile recorded with a biofluorescent characteristic. As adults their only predators are sharks, crocodiles, octopuses and some pelagic fish.

Appearance *The hawksbill sea turtle is different from other sea turtles in that it has an elongated, tapered head with a beak-like mouth - a hawksbill. On the front flippers they have two visible spiked claws on each flipper and prized patterned scutes on the shell.* **Size** *Adults grow to 1m, weighing in at around 80kg on average.*

Leatherback Sea Turtle

The largest of all sea turtles, these majestic creatures are considered globally vulnerable and, in the Pacific, are classed as critically endangered.

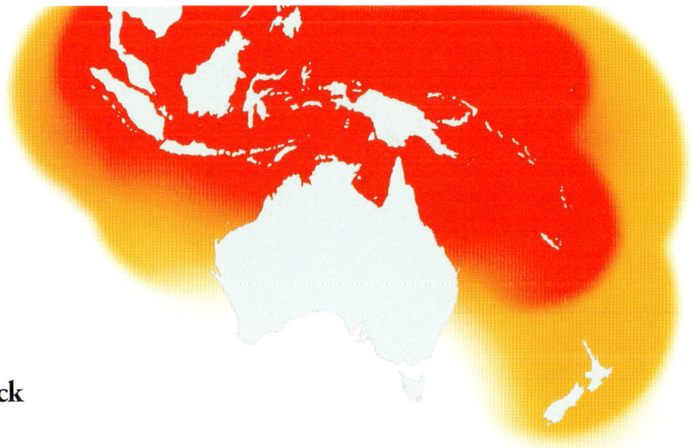

Often referred to as the **Lute Turtle** or **Leathery Turtle**, the **Leatherback Sea Turtle**, as its name suggests, has a leathery shell. Yes, it's rather soft, unlike the hard, rigid shells of most turtles. These critically endangered creatures are the considered the most seafaring and migratory of all the sea turtles, regularly crossing both the Atlantic and Pacific Oceans, consuming large quantities of jellyfish along the way. This helps keep the ocean jellyfish populations in check and is an important role in this aquatic ecosystem.

With worldwide distribution, **Leatherbacks** do visit Australian waters and, as global numbers have seriously declined in the last century, their plight is well recognised here. Decline has come as a result of intense egg collection, by-catch from nets, unsustainable fishing practices and simply the habit of consuming floating plastic pollution (a floating bag can look a lot like a jellyfish) - these giants of the sea turtle world are in dire need of our help.

Appearance *Leatherbacks are blue grey with distinctive lighter nodes on their ridges. The largest living turtle and the fourth largest reptile, they typically weigh in at between 320 and 450kgs.* **Size** *Usually 1-2 m from head to tail, although the largest Leatherback ever discovered was 3 m and weighed over 900kgs.*

OPPOSITE PAGE
A couple of Hawksbill Sea Turtles hunt the shallow reef, while a silent sentient Leatherback glides between the deep outcrops of the coral lagoon.

Freshwater Turtles and Ocean Sea Snakes

Australia has 869 reptile species, 93% of which are endemic and unique to the continent. From freshwater streams, rivers and swamps, across the deserts, through our diverse rainforests to the outlying islands off our coasts, and snaking through the ocean forests of our country's extensive coral reefs, our reptiles inhabit some of the wildest and most ecologically fragile places in Australia.

One of the largest species of side-neck turtles in the world, the **White-throated Snapping Turtle**, grows to about 45cm in shell length. This species is almost entirely aquatic, rarely coming ashore, and feeds on the fruits and buds of riparian vegetation. Its survival depends on securing nesting sites free from egg-raiding foxes, flooding and destructive trampling by cattle. The damming of rivers, changes in river temperatures and flood events destabilising nesting sites all affect reproduction.

In Western Australia the **Western Swamp Turtle** is in decline as well, a consequence mostly of its greatly altered habitat. This critically endangered tortoise exists only in small fragmented populations. Changed waterways, extraction of groundwater, reduced rainfall due to climate change and introduced foxes are all threats to their survival.

In the glassy clear waters of Ashmore and Hibernia Reefs, off the north-west coast of Western Australia, the plight of two rare sea snakes, the **Leaf-scaled Sea Snake** and the **Short-nosed Sea Snake** has become critical. The **Leaf-scaled Sea Snake**, with an average length of 60cm, dark blackish-brown or purplish in colour with paler cross bands, has disappeared from Ashmore Reef, one of its two strongholds.

The slightly larger, venomous **Short-nosed Sea Snake** grows to 1m in length. This more slender species, with a small head and pointed snout, has similar coloration and banding to the **Leaf-scaled Sea Snake**. The main threat to both snakes appears to be habitat degradation. This is the result of severe bleaching events (killing off prey fish species) and sand encroachment. In 1998, during an El Niño event, the effective Ashmore Reef ecosystem was reduced by 80%, demonstrating the fragility of our reef systems.

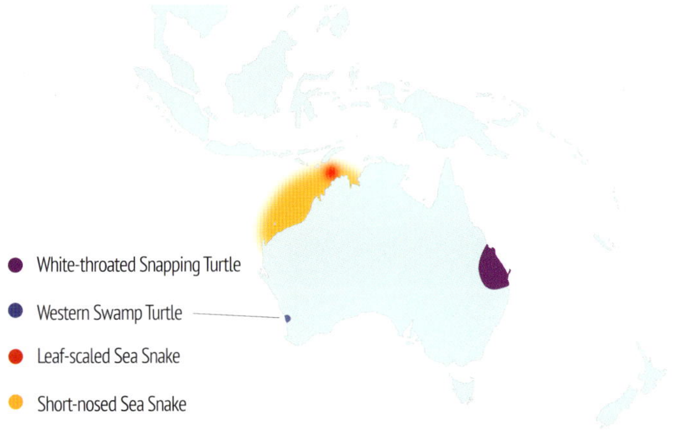

THIS PAGE
Top; the Leaf-scaled Sea Snake and **bottom;** the Short-nosed Sea Snake both share the same reef systems and the same dangers to their exsistence.

OPPOSITE PAGE
Left; the White-throated Snapping Turtle and **right;** The Western Swamp Turtle.

THIS PAGE
From the top; Lister's Gecko, The Blue-tailed Skink and Christmas Island Whiptail Forest Skink, below a Nangur Spiny Skink mother.

Below left to right; is featured the burrowing Skink-like creature, Allan's Lerista and the Eared Worm-lizard form Ouyen in Victoria.

Australia's Endangered Lizards

The world of sun-basking reptiles, elite nocturnal hunters adorned with colourful patterns and unique adaptions for life amongst rainforest trees, thicket and leaf litter, rocks and crevices, seems idyllic. However, some of these reptiles live on the knife-edge of extinction. Human impacts have opened some serious cracks in the eco-citadels of these wonderful lizards, including here in Australia. But as ever in nature there's always hope - only time will tell.

The rainforest trees of Christmas Island were once abundant with a small, tree-dwelling gecko, the **Lister's Gecko**, a patterned brown reptile growing to about 5cm. They scampered through the trees eating insects and other small invertebrates. However, introduced predators decimated their populations and none remain in the wild today. They are, however, part of a successful breeding programme to bring them back from extinction, which holds the promise of reintroducing these geckos to their original habitat soon.

Another Christmas Island resident, the **Christmas Island Blue-tailed Skink** or simply **Blue-tailed Skink**, is a delicate, slender lizard also once widespread on the island, foraging during the middle of the day, feeding on insects and other small invertebrates. This skink has a brown body but a striking light blue tail. This is thought to draw a predator's attention away from the rest of the body, and if it is caught by the tail it can lose it and escape. Despite this trick, introduced predators have ravaged the population and, like the gecko, this skink is now extinct in the wild, although breeding in captivity.

The **Christmas Island Forest Skink** or **Whiptail Skink** is also completely gone from the wild and was presumed extinct in 2017, a captive programme not being in place. There is perhaps some hope (the final declaration may take years to be officially made), but if true this represents Australia's first reptile extinction since European colonisation. The tales of these skinks indicates that the importance of our efforts in captive breeding and rewilding ecosystems - although almost a last resort - is more critical than ever.

The **Nangur Spiny Skink** gives us some hope in the fight against extinction. It was first discovered only in 1992 in south-east Queensland, living in semi-evergreen vine thicket and vine forest, an exciting new discovery in the herpetological world. A second colony was found 40km to the west in 1997. Genetic analysis indicates these populations became isolated from each other well over one million years ago, despite being such a short distance apart!

Endangered Curiosities

Sliders with no fore-limbs and legless Worm-lizards must be the strangest of our reptilian curiosities we have in Australia.

The **Retro Slider** or **Allan's Lerista** is a burrowing skink. It is grey or grey brown with darker-edged scales. Its sides are pale, underside whitish, with scales finely spotted dark brown. It has no fore limbs, but has single digit hind limbs and grows to 9cm in length.

But this strange, unique creature is not alone on the list of endangered sliders. The **Mallee Worm-lizard**, or **Eared Worm-lizard**, was originally discovered in the Woomelang and Ouyen areas of north-western Victoria. It inhabits shrub-land and open heath, primarily mallee country: specifically, unburnt scrub that hasn't seen fire for 40 years or more. Settlers and farmers, uprooting mallee roots, have unfortunately contributed to this legless lizard's endangered species status, although there have been some relatively recent discoveries of this curious creature, with colonies identified near Millicent, South Australia. Since 2012 annual surveys have expanded our knowledge of these fascinating bush creatures - and so hopefully our ability to help them survive.

Handfish of Hobart and Tropical Gobies

One of the earliest settlements in Australia was on the shores of the Derwent estuary, feeding into the Port of Hobart. It's Australia's second oldest port, gateway to the Antarctic and an active fishing port. This coastal settlement affected almost all of Derwent's saltmarsh wetlands and it has changed the ecology of the aquatic estuary environment forever. For many species below the surface of the harbour it's do or die. This is where the future of the world's rarest fish now rests in our hands.

There are four known handfish, all extremely rare. In fact, sadly, the **Pink Handfish** and **Ziebell's Handfish** are presumed extinct: the **Pink Handfish** has only ever been seen in the wild a few times and the **Ziebell's Handfish** hasn't been seen in over a decade. The other two, the **Red Handfish** and the **Spotted Handfish**, are listed as Critically Endangered. Unique to southern Tasmania, these handfish are faced with increasing levels of habitat loss, pollution, impacts associated with invasive species and climate change. There is some good news: recent dives and research have found a new tiny new population of distinctly different **Red Handfish**, which means there's a bigger gene pool for securing their survival. Plus, there may potentially be other populations out there. The **Spotted Handfish** was recently seen for the first time in 22 years, so it also seems to still be hanging in there.

Moving from the cold waters of the Derwent estuary to the warm tropical streams of north Queensland, we dive again into the fragile ecosystems of our waterways. **Opal Cling Gobies** are brightly coloured, finger-sized fish that populate the isolated shallow streams and torrents of the north. We have about ten different goby species in Australia. They grow to no more than 6cm and live in either streams or springs and disperse during rainfall events. These springs are refuges, affected little by drought and fed endlessly by the Great Artesian Basin.

The **Opal Cling Gobies**, as their name suggests, cling to rocks in streams, but two other critically endangered gobies, the **Edgbaston Goby** and the tiny **Elizabeth Springs Goby**, are found in only a handful of artesian springs in Queensland. In fact the latter is found only in marshy pools at Elizabeth Springs. The **Edgbaston Goby** is one of five related goby species but the **Elizabeth Springs Goby**, found 400km to the south west, has been ecologically and genetically marooned. The other gobies are located in South Australia and the Northern Territory. Ultimately, the future of these endangered fish is in our hands.

Derwent River Sea Star

Whether because of human impacts - sea and estuary temperature changes or pollutants from our industries - or other causes, the Derwent River Sea Star might have slipped into extinction on our watch.

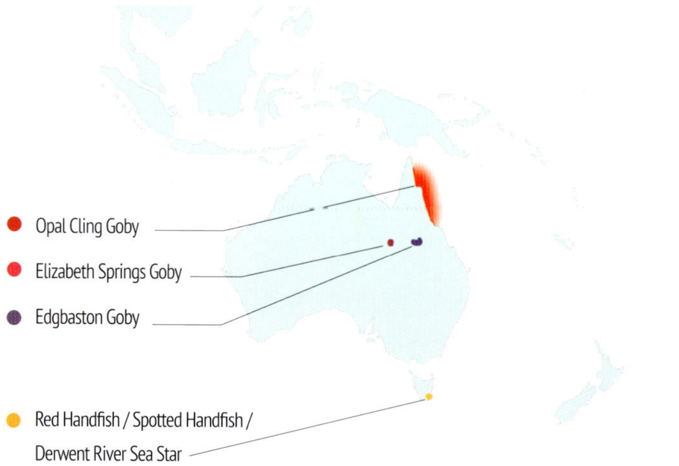

We often don't care to dip beneath the surface of things. Anything under the sea, in rockpools, in rivers or lakes is usually beyond our view. However, there is a great deal going on in these realms, hidden from our usual concern. Discovered half a century ago, not much is known about the **Derwent River Sea Star**. Science was only been able to study these rare sea stars for around 25 years. It was sighted, on and off, near the Tasman Bridge in Hobart, up until the early 1990s, but then came a notable decline in their numbers. Surveys in 1993 and 2010 failed to find a single individual and it was listed as Critically Endangered by the Tasmanian and Australian governments. But now, maybe it's time to say the **Derwent River Sea Star** is extinct. If this is the case, it's one of an alarming and growing number of Australian marine extinctions.

THIS PAGE

Top; Two rare Handfish, the Red Handfish and the whiter/paler Spotted Handfish.

Middle left; Derwent river Sea Star (also top corner).

Below top to bottom; Two Opal Cling Gobies above the brownish Elizabeth Springs Goby and the dappled blue/Brown Edgbaston Goby.

THIS PAGE
Top to bottom left to right; the Golden Galaxia, Clarance Galaxia, Barred Galaxia, Flathead Galaxia, Shaw Galaxia, Pedder Galaxia, Swan Galaxia and finally the largest minnon sized galaxiid fish, two Spotted Galaxias.

The Critically Endangered Galaxias

Many stories portrayed in this book are of tiny creatures or fragile ecosystems. The story of these Galaxias is probably no different! Yet if you are curious and fascinated by the diversity and rare beauty of Australia's flora and fauna it might be time to dive into the streams and rivers and discover more about our growing number of Critically Endangered Galaxias.

A new study has found that Australian freshwater fish face a high risk of extinction in the next 20 years. Many of these fish species are galaxias. From the large 20cm **Spotted Galaxia** down to small fingerling varieties, these fish live in many stream and river environments. The **Spotted Galaxia** seems to prefer still or slow flowing bodies of water at different elevations upland or close to the sea. It's usually found near the cover of fallen timber or rocks, in billabongs, lakes or near the edges of streams. Often called a **Native Spotted Mountain Trout**, **Trout Minnow**, or **Spotted Minnow**, it feeds mainly on aquatic and terrestrial insects. **Spotted Galaxias** also feed on crustaceans, waterbugs, midges and molluscs. Because they share the same diet as introduced trout, they compete for food, but even worse, the larger trout readily eat them. All galaxias are having difficulty competing with invasive carp, brown and rainbow trout and redfin.

The brownish-olive **Swan Galaxia**, endemic to a small region in eastern Tasmania, is now only found in the trout-free headwaters of the Swan and Macquarie Rivers, choosing to occupy shallow streams of low gradient.

Originally recorded only in Tasmania's Lake Pedder and its inflowing streams, the **Pedder Galaxia** has been officially considered to be extinct in the wild since 2005. After the Huon-Serpentine dam was built in 1972, its range grew initially into Lake Gordon and Wedge River. However, by the 1980s it was rarely captured and had disappeared in the wild by 1996.

The **Clarence Galaxia** is a scaleless, small galaxiid fish. It has a dark brown back with brown bars and bands extending down its sides, while the belly is a lighter yellow-cream color. The **Clarence Galaxia** is found only in central Tasmania, restricted to the Clarence and Nive River catchments. Six of the known populations are located in the headwaters of the Clarence River and a seventh population exists in a small headwater tributary of the Nive River.

The **Golden Galaxia**, like the the struggling **Clarence Galaxia** is endemic to central Tasmania. Again isolated, surviving wild populations, are only known to exist in two locations, Lake Sorrell and Lake Crescent.

The **Flathead Galaxia** is a freshwater fish found in lowland rivers and streams and associated billabongs, backwaters of the southern Murray-Darling river system. **Flathead Galaxia** like other native fish can migrate into upland habitats. Trout can also migrate upstream, into these areas, and they are proving to be exterminating many varieties of **Galaxias**.

The **Barred Galaxia**, a small, scaleless and non-migratory freshwater fish, is endemic to a small upland area in central Victoria. This stronghold falls within the Murray-Darling Basin side of the Great Dividing Range. The fish is found only in a few high alpine streams feeding the Goulburn River catchment.

The most imperilled fish species in Australia recently studied was the **Shaw Galaxia** — a tiny fish with tiger stripes now only found in one waterway in South Gippsland.

According to the study, the **Shaw Galaxia** has an 80% chance of becoming extinct within the next two decades if no conservation measures are put into place. The study also highlighted that a further thirteen galaxiid fish, including the **West Gippsland Galaxia**, **Tapered Galaxia**, **Dargo Galaxia**, **Morwell Galaxia**, **Mcdowall's Galaxia**, **Stocky Galaxia**, **Kosciuszko Galaxia**, **Yalmy Galaxia**, **East Gippsland Galaxia**, **Hunter Galaxia**, **Moroka Galaxia**, **Swan Galaxia** and **Short-tail Galaxia**, all have a 70% chance of becoming extinct within the next two decades if no conservation measures are put into place.

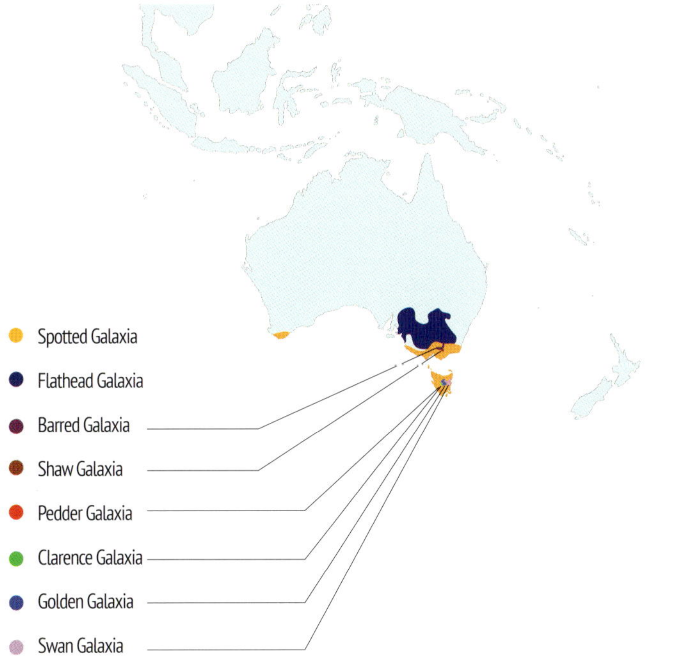

Rare River Sharks, Sawfish and The Grey Nurse

We often think we know all about sharks. But there are so many species and a lot we don't know. From the river-mouths of tropics there are rare and elusive river sharks and the strange and weird-looking Sawfish, that swing their saw-like nose to impale prey. In the southern waters off New South Wales the Grey Nurse Shark is also at risk. All these creatures have small ranges, unique breeding habits or not much is known. Nature has so many secrets. Sometimes we have to explore and discover these treasures, to give them more time in the fight against extinction.

The **Speartooth Shark** is a medium-sized whaler shark with small eyes, no distinctive colour pattern and a short broadly rounded snout. It gets its name from its slender, broadly separated, serrated upper teeth. Primarily fish-eaters that have adapted to hunting in cloudy estuarine river waters, the maximum size of these species is unknown, but they may grow to a length of 2-3 metres.

The **Northern River Shark** is very similar, although not a lot is known about this species. All we really understand is that it is scarce across its range and that encounters are very rare.

Sawfish or **Carpenter Sharks**, are a family of rays characterized by a long, narrow nose extension, lined with sharp exterior teeth that resembles a saw. They are among the largest river fish with some species reaching lengths of about 7–7.6 m similar to the Shovel-nose Sharks.

Sawfish are found worldwide in tropical and subtropical regions, always choosing coastal marine ecosystems with brackish estuarine waters or freshwater rivers and lakes. There are two species in Australia, the **Largetooth Sawfish** and the **Green Sawfish**, often named the **Olive Sawfish.** They should not be confused with 'Sawsharks' or even the marlin-like 'Swordfish', which have similar names but are very different. **Sawfish** have been known and hunted for thousands of years and play an important mythological and spiritual role in many Indigenous cultures.

Grey Nurse Sharks tend to live in shallower inshore waters, preferring habitats with sandy-bottomed gutters and large rocky caves. **Grey Nurse Sharks** are more active at night, feeding upon fish, smaller sharks, squid, crustaceans and rays.

Grey Nurse Sharks are unusual breeders. Mating mainly occurs in autumn and they birth live young in winter. Near the end of the gestation, the more fully developed embryos eat the all the smaller embryos and unfertilised eggs while still inside the bi-chambered womb. As a result, only two pups are produced every two years. This is the lowest reproductive rate of any shark, which makes this species so susceptible to a sudden population collapse.

There are two populations of **Grey Nurse Shark** in Australia - the east coast population and the west coast population. The east coast population is listed as Critically Endangered. A Fisheries survey in 2000 revealed that the number of sharks at that time could have been as low as 292 individuals.

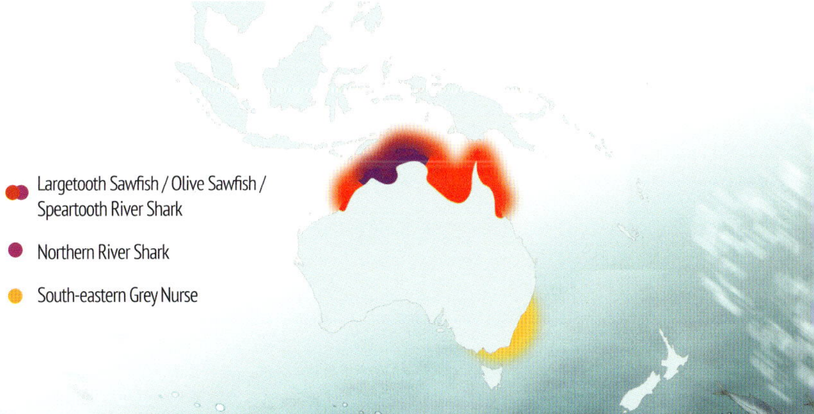

OPPOSITE PAGE
Two rare Speartooth River Sharks hunt the tropical brackish river waters. Two Olive Sawfish lift off the silt bottom and get out of their way, while a Largetooth Sawfish patrols the rocky riverbank. Below them all a rare Northern River Shark stalks the murky bottom.

THIS PAGE
Several Grey Nurse Sharks hunt the sandy south-eastern reefs for fish and stingrays.

The Murray Darling River System

Murray Cod populations have declined severely since European colonisation. There are a number of causes, including severe overfishing, introduced fish like the invasive carp, river regulation and habitat loss. They once inhabited the entire Murray-Darling basin in huge numbers, growing to the size of large groupers. However, after years of water degradation they are now a listed as an Endangered species.

The Murray-Darling basin in eastern Australia is the largest and most important river system in Australia, a catchment capturing around 14% of the continent's water. The **Murray Cod's** natural range encompasses nearly the whole Murray-Darling basin, particularly the lowland floodplains, but extending well into upland tributaries. The fish is an important part of this river system and also a significant part of our first Australians' culture.

The **Murray Cod** is the largest exclusively freshwater fish in Australia, an apex predator and one of the largest freshwater fish in the world. It hunts and eats almost anything smaller than itself. They truly are a mighty fish and worth protecting.

Appearance *A large grouper-like fish, the Murray Cod has a deep, elongated body. Round and robust, it has a broad, scooped head and a large mouth lined with pads of very small, needle-like teeth. Its dappled yellowish-green to green camouflage pattern creates a kind of marbled appearance, like a leopard's markings. It has a white to cream underbelly.* **Size** *Murray cod are large fish, with adults reaching 80–100cm. Some grow over 1m long and the largest on record was over 1.8m and about 113kg in weight.*

Widespread throughout the Murray–Darling Basin, including the Murrumbidgee and Molonglo rivers, **Silver Perch** share the waterways with the **Murray Cod**. They are listed as Critically Endangered nationally, Vulnerable in NSW, Threatened in Victoria and Protected in both South Australia and parts of Queensland. They have not been recorded within the ACT since 1988. Introduced species, such as carp and redfin compete for food and prey on juveniles. **Silver Perch** are artificially bred in hatcheries for fish stocking, fish markets and are used to stock our drinking reservoirs. In the wild, **Silver Perch** consume aquatic plants, algae, molluscs, crustaceans and insect larvae.

Appearance *A moderate to large fish with a strongly compressed oval body covered in small, thin scales and small head* **Size** *They usually grow to 30–40cm long.*

We now jump from the monstrous **Murray Cod** to the tiny **Red-finned Blue-eye**. This is only found in the group of natural springs at Edgbaston Reserve in central western Queensland. These springs are part of a large inland drainage basin that runs to Lake Eyre and is part of the Great Artesian Basin that underlies much of central Australia.

At only 3cm long, **Red-finned Blue-eyes** are easily overlooked as unimportant. However, the tiny remaining wild population of these diminutive fish found in this artesian spring is vital to the health of these unique and fragile ecosystems. The introduced and highly invasive Mosquito Fish is the biggest threat to the **Red-finned Blue-eye's** survival, although such a fragile habitat can also easily be ravaged by cattle, feral pigs and drought.

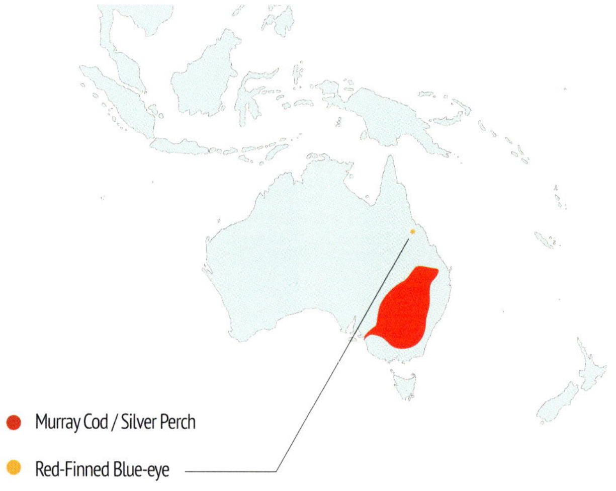

OPPOSITE PAGE
King of the river: a large Murry Cod floats under a large snag and tangled debris of logs. Ready to ambush their prey, three Silver Perch hang around the cod, possibly for protection.

THIS PAGE
Two tiny Red-finned Blue-eyes.

Southern Blue-fin Tuna

In Australia, 95% of the Southern Blue-fin Tuna are caught in the Great Australian Bight. Fishing for these creatures was immortalised in an Australian kids' book *Blue Fin*, written in 1969 by Colin Thiele and nearly a decade later adapted to the big screen. If ever there was a fish that best illustrates how wrong the way we fish is, then Southern Blue-fin Tuna fishing is up there with the "longlining" of sharks and European "deep sea trawling". Today, Southern Blue-fin Tuna are listed as Critically Endangered and population levels are still declining, yet fishing continues.

We eat loads of tuna, it's great for our health! So why is **Southern Blue-fin Tuna** on the Critically Endangered list? Firstly, you have to detangle yourself from the romantic notions of fishing and realise it's a question of diversity. All tuna is not the same, and understanding how we bring tuna to your plate is important. Large scale fishing often has a dramatic environmental impact on wild pollulations.

Southern Blue-fin Tuna doesn't end up as canned or tinned tuna. It's a gourmet food. It doesn't end up spooned out over pasta or salad. Yes! It's not that stinky kind in your friend's lunch box. But if you have ever eaten sushi - Bingo! You are starting to get the difference.

Our **Southern Blue-fin Tuna** is in high demand for use in Japanese cuisine. A prized ingredient in sashimi and sushi, it has a fresh delicious, mild flavour and that melt-in-your mouth velverty flesh. Popularity worldwide has increased demand for these sleek giants of our southern oceans. Apart from the worldwide appetite and our healthy hunger for this fish, culturally in Australia we just love our sport and recreational fishing. Emotionally, we don't see the pressures we put on nature. Besides most people can't really tell the difference between **Yellow-fin Tuna** and **Southern Blue-fin Tuna** unless they are deeply passionate about fish, fish for a living or are ecologists.

As a nation, we like to fish and to support our fishing industries, but somewhere we must find a balance or else we may lose this fish altogether. Just as the poem and movie *The Man from Snowy River* romanticizes the pioneering heritage of the invasive brumby in the high country, so *Blue Fin*, a coming of age story, romanticizes the courage of the tuna fleets out of Port Lincoln. These same fleets have reduced tuna populations by 80% across the last five decades and they are still declining, even after we have tried to ethically change our ways. However, we are heading in the right direction to save our fisheries, and fishing practices have improved somewhat since the 1960s, partly in response to over-fishing and trying to reach sustainable quotas. New catch limits mean our **Southern Blue-fin Tuna** haul is down since the 1950s. This sounds like a great thing, yet the change has created another alarming problem.

Today, most **Southern Blue-fin Tuna** are caught as juveniles for farming in "aquaculture". The targeting and taking of up to 95% of these pre-spawning wild fish out of the ocean, out of their natural life cycle, makes it extremely difficult to rebuild future wild stocks and restore the oceans to their original pre-fishing levels.

The vastness of the ocean and the romantic ideals of our right to this resource cloud our path to realistic conservation. However, we must begin to work with nature, seek to protect it and restore the balance. We urgently need to look out for these dwindling numbers of **Southern Blue-fin Tuna**, so as to maintain that diversity in our oceans. Even though we can't often fathom what goes on below the surface of our oceans, sustaining diversity is the key to the health of any ecosystem.

Appearance *There are many types of tuna worldwide and in Australia a lot of people can't distinguish between the more common Yellow-fin Tuna and the endangered Southern Blue-fin Tuna. Specifically, the Southern Blue-fin has a pectoral fin and the silver underside is marked with white dots and uneven lines. The second dorsal fin is a mix of grey and yellow in colour. The tail fin is dark blue.* **Size** *Southern Blue-fin Tuna are ocean giants. They grow to over 2m in length and weigh a whopping 260kg as adults.*

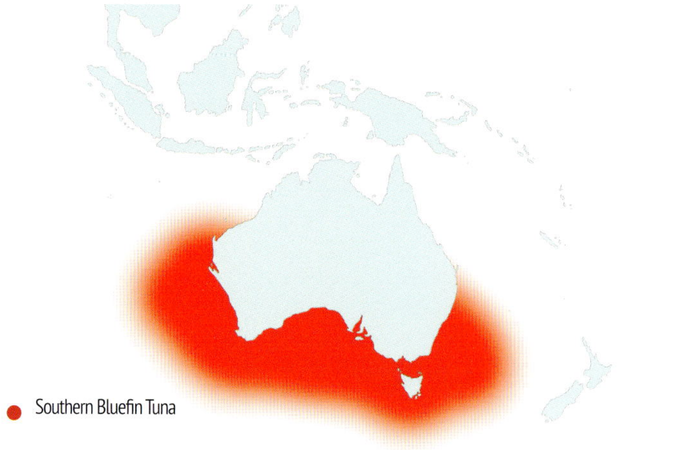

THIS PAGE
Wild Southern Blue-fin Tuna Chase down their daily food in the Great Australian Bight.

From a Tassie Giant to our Burrowing Crayfish

Protected since 1998, the Tasmanian Giant Freshwater Crayfish is a monster. Usually growing to 30-40cm in length and 2kg in weight, they are as big - if not bigger - than our unique Hairy Marron. Living to 60 years of age or older, these crayfish have been reported up to 80cm long and 6kg - now that's a giant!

Our **Tasmanian Giant Freshwater Crayfish**, also called the Tasmanian Giant Freshwater Lobster, is quite possibly the largest freshwater crayfish in the world. An omnivorous crustacean, it will eat decaying wood, leaves and microbes, small fish, insects and rotting animal flesh. Found in the northern Tasmanian rivers this crayfish is listed as Endangered, due to habitat degradation and overfishing (although it has been prohibited to catch these giants for over two decades).

In comparison, our smallest freshwater crayfish, from sub-tropical eastern Australia, near Toonumbar National Park, is the **Orange-bellied Crayfish.** This tiny, yabby-like arthropod grows up to a full body length of 10cm, with the female being smaller. These crustaceans are elusive and shy, spending most of their time within their burrows.

Not all crayfish live in streams and riverbanks, however! Let's investigate the very specialised, land-based burrowing crayfish. They live in tunnel systems in muddy banks, seepages and peaty areas in swamps and on heath and flood plains. They make visible mud chimneys of soil pellets that are expelled at the burrow entrances as they dig.

These curious little arthropods are listed as Critically Endangered, threatened by a range of human impacts. These are primarily clearing for pasture, plantations and other conversions to their habitat, and the lowering of the water table as a result of agricultural and forestry activities. Downstream effects of quarrying and road construction, trampling of habitat by stock (crushing crayfish or their burrows) and inappropriate fire management have also had a broad impact on these crustaceans. These are the Endangered arthropods found around Australia: the **Scottsdale Burrowing Crayfish**, found north of Scottsdale in north-east Tasmania; the **Central North Burrowing Crayfish** found near Devonport; the **Dunsborough Burrowing Crayfish** and **Margaret River Burrowing Crayfish** of Western Australia (with narrow geographical ranges on the coast); the **Mallacoota Burrowing Crayfish** and the **Warragul Burrowing Crayfish**, both endemic to Victoria, but little is known about these bush creatures.

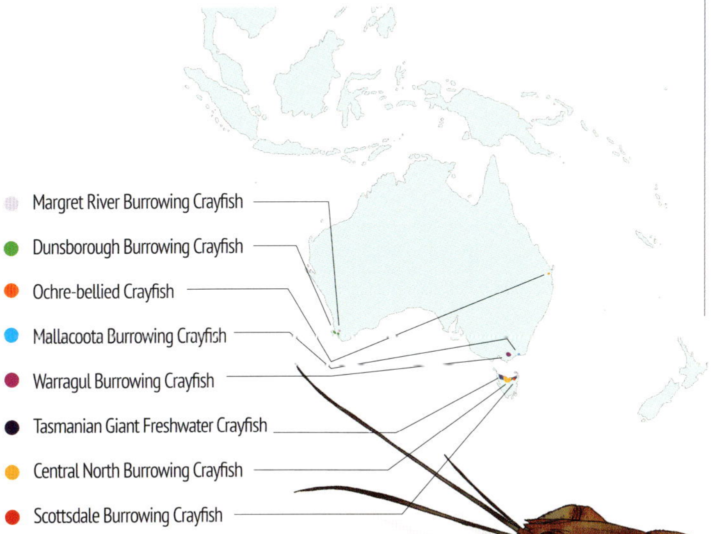

OPPOSITE PAGE
Two Tasmanian Giant Freshwater Crayfish hunt on the river bed.

THIS PAGE
Left; The tiny Ochre-bellied Crayfish.

Six burrowing arthropods featured far right from top to bottom; Margaret River Burrowing Crayfish, Mallacoota Burrowing Crayfish, Scottsdale Burrowing Crayfish, Central North Burrowing Crayfish, and the biggest looking being the 10cm long Warragul Burrowing Crayfish and Dunsborough Burrowing Crayfish.

Margaret River Hairy Marron

It wasn't so long ago that Australian kids used to catch yabbies in dams and creeks. Like all great fishing stories 'the bigger is often better'. The Margaret River Hairy Marron, one of the world's largest freshwater crayfish, is no little yabby catch! Now very rare, this fascinating species is endemic to the upper regions of Margaret River in Western Australia. As an iconic creature, there is solid conservation focus and it is hoped that this will be a tale of recovery and survival - that it will survive for many generations to come.

The **Margaret River Hairy Marron** is indeed one of the largest freshwater crayfish on the planet, reaching over 38cm in length and a good 2kg in weight. Living in the clean, clear waters of the upper reaches of the Margaret River system, they survive on small organisms.

Like some other Australian crayfish, they are pretty comfortable on land for a short period of time and do not need to burrow into the river beds to escape drought. These marron have been an important food source for the local Noongar people for thousands of years. Today, however, it is estimated that the population has decreased by up to 90%, with only an estimated 10,000 individuals remaining in the wild.

There are many factors threatening the survival of these **Hairy Marrons**. Common introduced Smooth Marron breed with the **Hairy Marron**, diluting their genetics. Invasive species of fish, namely the Mosquito Fish and Redfin Perch, compete for food. Yabbies have moved in from other catchments too. Recent surveys also haven't ruled out changes to water volumes, temperature and flow; factors that could be critical to the **Hairy Marron's** current stability and future recovery.

Appearance *Tufts of hair-like bristles growing on its carapace, the shell or other body surfaces, distinguish the Hairy from the commoner Smooth Marron. This unique "hairy" feature resulted in its recognition as a separate species in 2002. The Hairy Marron has black pincers and an olive-green or brown shell, with areas of red or purple on the underside of females.* **Size** *Reaching over 38cm in length and 2kg in weight.*

Glenelg Freshwater Mussels

The Glenelg Freshwater Mussel is a sedentary, bivalve mollusc found only in the lower reaches of the Crawford River, a tributary of the larger Glenelg River, in south-west Victoria.

The Gunditj Mirring, traditional peoples of the area, say the mussels used to be plentiful and widespread. A couple of specimens at the Australian Museum are said to have been collected from as far off as Port Fairy. What has put the **Glenelg Freshwater Mussel** on the Endangered list is its loss of primary habitat through erosion, siltation and damage to protective riverbank vegetation, caused by grazing stock.

These mussels prefer the shallower parts of the river, although these areas can be prone to drying out (during low flows, the mussels can follow the receding waters, burrowing into the mud for survival). Losing riverbank shrubs removes shade in the shallow areas, increasing water temperatures, in turn promoting unfavourable algal blooms. Also, less shrubs means less debris which means less refuge for the mussels. Other potential threats to the species are pesticide use and predation by invasive carp.

Appearance *The shell is strong and almond-shaped with a rounded rear border and a surface marked with fine sculpture (wrinkles). The periostracum - or flaky shell covering - is olive-green in immature individuals and dark purple-brown in mature individuals.* **Size** *Glenelg Freshwater Mussels reach 51–80mm in length.*

THIS PAGE

Top; Two Margret River Hairy Marrons in the shallow upland reaches of the Margret River, WA.

Below; Depicted on a similar creek-bed, The Glenelg Freshwater Mussels filter food in the lower tributaries of the Glenelg River.

Greater Gliders

There are three species of Greater Glider inhabiting eucalypt forests along our Eastern seaboard. These majestic nocturnal feeders glide through the arboreal skyscrapers, feeding off the flowering canopy. While all gliders are in decline, the Victorian species of the central highlands is considered endangered, due to logging and habitat loss. Their survival is dependent on the last remaining old growth forests.

Originally considered one, **Greater Gliders** are now known to be three species: the **Northern**, **Central** and **Southern Greater Gliders**. Strangely, they are more closely related to the Ring-tail Possum than say Sugar Gliders. They vary in size from the slightly smaller **Northern Glider** to the largest, cat-sized **Southern Glider**. Primarily nocturnal, foraging high in the forest canopy at night, by day these gliders rest in hollowed trees, lined with leaves and bark. To avoid natural predators like the **Powerful Owl**, they rotate between up to 20 different dens within their territory.

Greater Gliders live almost entirely on young leaves and flowering eucalypt buds. They are beautiful bush creatures and a thrill to observe or glimpse while spotlighting. Ultimately, their survival comes down to the preservation and health of their native forest home.

Appearance *Greater gliders are large marsupials. Quite possum-like in appearance, their bodies are covered with a shaggy coat of fur. They have short heads with pointed muzzles and are known for their large ears, fringed and backed with long fuzzy fur.* **Size** *Greater Gliders grow to about 40cm from head to body with a tail adding another 45cm. Females are generally larger than the males.*

Leadbeater's Possum

The rare beauty of the Victorian central highlands is home to the shy, elusive and critically endangered Leadbeater's Possum.

The Victorian State faunal emblem and once thought to be extinct, a colony of Leadbeater's Possums was discovered in 1961, and the fight to maintain and grow this wild population has been a matter of community pride. This marsupial omnivore (once called the fairy possum) feeds on sap, nectar, lerps, insects and arthropods. Bushfires have often devastated colonies, exacerbating ongoing habitat loss through logging. Feral cats are an added threat to these adorable creatures, of which only an estimated 2,000 remain in the wild.

Appearance *This beautifully marked possum is a tiny, nocturnal creature with large eyes and a long tail.* **Size** *Measures around 30cm in total length.*

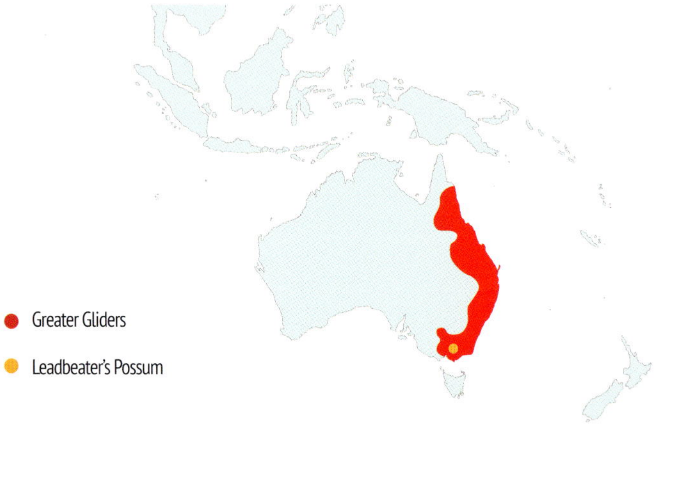

THIS PAGE
Two Southern Greater Gliders in the moonlight, enjoying the giant Mountain Ash forest

OPPOSITE PAGE
The Victorian Emblem, three Leadbeater's Possums forage for insects.

Mountain Pygmy-Possum

The unique Mountain Pygmy-possum, the largest of the Australian Pygmy-possums, is restricted to a specialised alpine habitat and was once thought to be extinct. They were rediscovered at Mt Hotham in the 1960s. Even with conservation efforts, there are fewer than 2,000 left in the wild.

Australia's only hibernating marsupial, living off fat stores, the **Mountain Pygmy-possum** hibernates for up to seven months under the snow. Critically endangered, at present there are only three known populations, living in alpine rocks and boulders in the Bogong High Plains, from Mt Buller in Victoria to Mt Kosciuzko in New South Wales.

Loss of habitat, climate change, threats from feral cats and foxes, plus other human impacts are all pushing this unique **Pygmy-possum** to the brink of extinction. Feeding on insects, fleshy fruits, nuts, nectar and seeds, the possum's key food source over spring, the Bogong Moth, has drastically declined in numbers and this may be another threat to its long-term survival. This alpine bush creature is now part of a captive breeding programme led by zoos in Victoria and New South Wales. Rewilding and ongoing conservation programmes, with a little bit of luck and support, will eventually see the down-listing of these adorable little possums.

Appearance *Its body is covered in a thick coat of fine grey or brown fur except for its stomach, which is cream. Its tail is hairless. The female has a pouch with four teats.* **Size** *At almost 14cm its prehensile tail is longer than its combined head and body length.*

Other Small Marsupials and Native Mice

Open forest, mallee scrub, eucalypt woodlands abundant with sedge, grass, heath, fungi and ferns, places filled with littered understorey, often along creek lines, rocky ridges, cracked craggy outcrops, moist swamps or in bush gullies: all will be the home of an array of small marsupials and native mice.

Australia has an estimated 250 marsupial species and around 60 species of rodents or small mice across the whole continent. Since European colonisation and the introduction of invasive feral pests, Australia's small, endemic species of native marsupials and mice have been slowly declining. Feral and domestic dogs, cats, foxes may hunt them, and non-native rats and mice now compete with them for food and habitat. What habitat there is, is diminishing due to farming, mining and urban sprawl. Animals like the **Silver-Headed Antechinus**, the **Hastings River Mouse** and the **Smoky Mouse** are rarely seen and have become Critically Endangered.

The rare marsupial **Kangaroo Island Dunnart**, in South Australia, is a good example of how island fauna is particularly vulnerable to new threats. Their small, limited range and local specialisations make them very vulnerable to invasive pests and sensitive to habitat destruction.

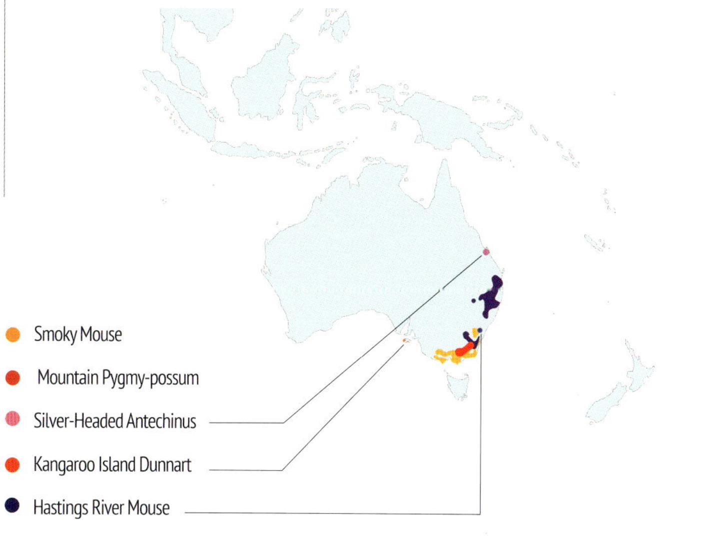

OPPOSITE PAGE

Above; depicted in an Alpine heathland, high on the Bogong Plains, these two Mountain Pygmy-possums are out in springtime, foraging at dusk.

Below, clockwise from top left; two elusive and endangered Hastings River Mice, the Silver-headed Antechinus (on a rock), the Kangaroo Island Dunnart and the Smoky Mouse.

Hairy-nosed Wombats and the Woylie

While there are many factors that cause populations to collapse, each of these species offers a different perspective on a familiar recurring problem. Common Wombats are robust, plentiful and their adaptability to different habitats creates a wide distribution. However, the two subspecies of Hairy-nosed Wombat, the Northern and the Southern, are both pretty picky with their lodgings. With reducing potential habitats and preferring sandy soils, these wombats have became isolated. Yet a wide territory isn't always the best strategy in the survival game. The Woylie roamed over 60% of Australia before European settlement and the introduction of the red fox. This invasive species used the Woylie's vast numbers and range to help adapt to the Australian desert and spread out to dominate the arid red centre.

Our **Northern Hairy-nosed Wombats** look quite distinct from their cousins and have different burrowing habits to their wombat ancestors. They used to range from Queensland to Victoria and only in the last 100 years has their population declined rapidly. The **Southern Hairy-nosed Wombat**, the smallest of our wombat species, is scattered across areas of semi-arid scrub and mallee from the eastern Nullarbor Plain to north-western New South Wales. It has the same fussiness, preferring sandy soil burrows and, like its northern cousin, a particular diet of native grasses - which in the last century have been overrun and out-matched by introduced grass species.

The changing ecology of their home ranges was the first thing to cause these wombats' numbers to decline, making both subspecies vulnerable. The **Northern Hairy-nosed Wombat** suffered a range of threats before its population collapsed. Widespread farming started to upset the balance, while predation by packs of wild dogs (the wombat's primary predator), competition for food from invasive rabbits, diseases from fungus in the changing soil, plus floods, droughts and wildfires also contributed to their severe habitat loss, eventually reducing their range to 300 hectares of the Epping National Forest in east-central Queensland. While the **Southern Hairy-nosed Wombats** aren't endangered across the Nullarbor Plains in South Australia, the New South Wales populations are considered endangered and in decline. Understanding these two species' stories is important: similar issues threaten both the **Northern** and **Southern** species and now all populations live in small, highly localised ranges, making them especially vulnerable to natural disasters. The **Northern** cousins have been on the Critically Endangered list for a while. The only plus side to this is that huge efforts have been made to understand their fragility, protect them and try to recover this precious lone population.

The size of a rabbit, the **Woylie**, or **Brush-tailed Bettong**, is a marsupial that digs at night for fungi on the roots of shrubs and trees, usually foraging close to its central nest. It's found in many habitats, including low arid scrub and dry desert spinifex grasslands. It was common and widely spread throughout the mainland interior of Australia until around 1912 when it started to disappear.

In 1927 Europeans introduced the red fox. The foxes used the **Woylie** and other small marsupials as a food source as they spread out and bred across the arid interior. The foxes, along with increasing numbers of feral cats, were most likely the main cause of the **Woylie** population collapse. Yet there are always other factors, such as the rising numbers of rabbits competing for food. Grazing cattle, sheep, wheat crops and western farming methods also probably turned their world upside down. By 1950 most of the northern and eastern **Woylie** populations were extinct. Luckily, some small **Woylie** colonies have persisted until today in south-west Australia, surviving while similar mammals like the **Lesser Bilby**, **Desert Bandicoot**, **Pig-footed Bandicoot** and others have disappeared over the last century. The reason for this might just be similar to the **Numbat** story - another very cute and curious native survivor.

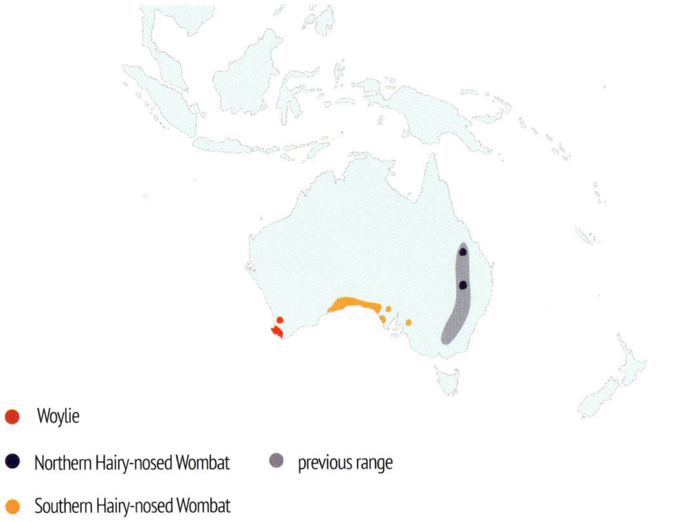

THIS PAGE
The Northern Hairy-nosed Wombat rambles through the arid scrub followed by the smaller, but more robust Southern Hairy-Nosed Wombat. Two foraging Woylies or Brush-Tailed Bettongs prepare to hop out of the way.

THIS PAGE
Clockwise from top; Building a nest, the White-tipped Stick-nest Rat; the Bramble Cay Mosaic-tailed Rat; the Carpentarian Rock-rat (on a log); the MacDonnell Range Rock-rat or Central Rock-rat; two round grey-coated Broad-toothed Rock Rats.

Ground dwelling Native Rats

Australia has around 60 species of native rodents, including eight species of common native rat that evolved from ancestors which arrived around a million years ago. A handful of these are endangered, one has been confirmed to have become extinct in the last decade and several others are on the edge of extinction.

To make the idea of rats more reader-friendly, let's start with the **White-tipped Stick-nest Rat** or **Lesser Stick-nest Rat**, which is presumed extinct. It lived in central Australia where it built nests of sticks that accumulated over years, becoming very large. The last confirmed sighting was in 1933, although a credible report in 1970 suggested that it may still have been surviving in remote unsurveyed territory. The often ever-moving, ever-changing scale of Threatened species classifications can confuse many young naturalists. Listed Critically Endangered in 2008, our **Stick-nest Rat** had its status revised back to Extinct again in 2016.

The **Bramble Cay Melomys**, or **Bramble Cay Mosaic-tailed Rat**, was a native Australian rodent on small Bramble Cay, a tiny island in the Torres Strait. In 2019 the government declared it Extinct, although it probably disappeared between 2009-2011. Endemic to Bramble Cay, it's officially regarded as the first mammal extinction due to climate change.

Cattle grazing, habitat loss, and introduced foxes and cats are the major reasons for a native rodent population to collapse, and have pushed all of our next three native rats close to extinction: the **Carpentarian Rock-rat**, found in isolated rainforests in the gorge systems of our gulf country; the **Central Rock-rat**, also known as the **Central Thick-tailed Rock-rat** or **MacDonnell Range Rock-rat**, of the MacDonnell Ranges; and the **Broad-toothed Rat** of the wet alpine and sub-alpine heaths of Kosciuszko National Park.

There maybe less than 30,000 Black-footed Tree-rats left in the wild.

Black-footed Tree rat

The endangered **Black-footed Tree-rat** ranges from the savannahs of Cape York Peninsula in Queensland west to the Kimberley region of Western Australia. Tropical woodland habitat or open forest are suitable country for this tree rat. Its already sparse population has been reduced by 50% in the last decade.

Appearance *This tree rat has a greyish-brown coat of shaggy, coarse fur and has a creamy underbelly. The hind feet are black with well developed pads and sharp claws. They have large ears, a long tail, with a brush of white hair at the end.* **Size** *The height of the rat is typically 25-31cm with a length of 32-42cm.*

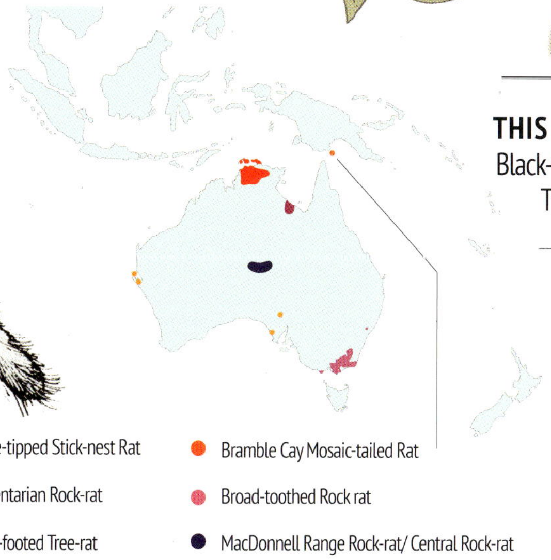

THIS PAGE Black-footed Tree-rat

THIS PAGE Christmas Island Flying-foxes.

An Island Flying-fox

Island Flying-foxes roost in lush rainforest trees in groups ('camps') of up to several hundred.

Endemic to Christmas Island, the **Christmas Island Flying-fox** is one of the few species of bats that are active during the day and they are often seen flying and foraging during the mid-afternoon. These **Flying-foxes** eat fruit and blossoms, including the flowers of the island's coconut palms.

The main threats to these **Flying-foxes** are the loss of feeding trees and roosting habitat. Add to this the effects of phosphate mining and several invasive species, including the Barking Gecko, Oriental Wolf-snake, African Snail, Black Rat, feral cat, Yellow Crazy-ants and a Tanzanian centipede. The smaller, stressed colony is now also more vulnerable to population loss from natural gale-force storm winds, which can sweep bats off to sea. The population has declined sharply, reducing by 75% between 1984-2006 and a further 39% from 2006-2012.

Appearance *A medium-sized bat, males are slightly heavier than females. Males reach peak body mass in May, coinciding with the mating season. It has a broad snout, short-pointed ears, and teeth specific to its diet. Covered in deep shining black fur, the body is slightly browner at the head.* **Size** *averaging 250–500g on average, males are slightly bigger than females.*

Beautiful Little Bats

In Australia we have some of the most biodiverse ecosystems on the planet, although it's a harsh and often unforgiving place at times. Most of our fauna are used to these challenges, yet we have the world's highest extinction rate.

Let's consider the **Bare-rumped Sheathtail Bat**, a species that has not been sighted in Australia for many years. Found in caves, tree hollows and between rocks they roost together in colonies, though hang apart from each other. **Bare-rumped Sheathtail Bats** were so named because they have very little hair on their hips. Population declines were due to loss of roost sites by mining, logging and agriculture plus overall human disturbance.

The **Lord Howe Island Long-eared Bat** was known only from a skull found on Lord Howe Island in 1972. An insectivorous species with long-ears and elongated head, we know almost next to nothing else about these bats. They may have been observed during the twentieth century, but are likely to have become extinct since shipwrecks introduced rats and large owls were then introduced to control the rats.

Back on Christmas Island, the **Christmas Island Pipistrelle** is now presumed extinct. The last individual was sighted in 2009, with no further sightings despite efforts to locate them.

The **Southern Bent-wing Bat** is a tiny microbat, measuring 52-58mm long with dark reddish brown fur on its back and a distinctive domed forehead. It eats a variety of insects and moths, like many bats using echolocation whilst flying and feeding. Cave-dependent, it is found in south-western Victoria, only using caves with a suitable specific micro-climate. It is listed as Critically Endangered.

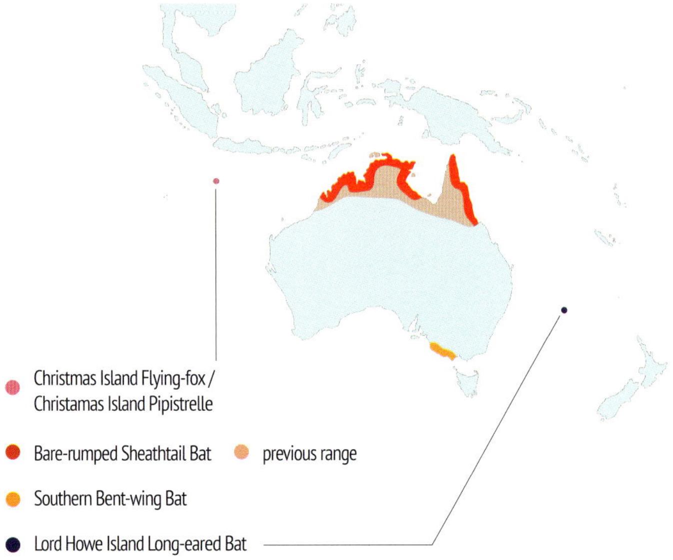

THIS PAGE

Top left; A Southern Bent-wing Bat in flight.

Top right; A Bare-rumped Sheathtail Bat chasing prey.

Bottom left; A Lord Howe Island Long-eared Bat.

Bottom right; Two tiny Christmas Island Pipistrelles, one in flight and the other clinging to limb.

THIS PAGE

Bottom; two silvery coated Gilbert's Potoroos hunt in the coastal forest understory.

Top left; you can see brown coloured pelt of two Long-footed Potoroos with one hiding.

Top right; The distinctive banding of a couple of Eastern Barred Bandicoots foraging in the Banksia forests of South-eastern Victoria.

Gilberts Potoroo and Long-footed Potoroo

From the thick scrub and heath-covered coastal dunes of Two Peoples Bay Nature Reserve in Western Australia to the national parks of Sydney, our coastline still has a few safe refuges for two species of endangered Potoroos. The small grey Gilbert's Potoroo in the west and the Long-footed Potoroo in the east are now, however, rare sights.

Once considered extinct, **Gilbert's Potoroo** is a small rat-kangaroo found on the Western Australian south coast, growing to 20-23cm in length. In 1994, at Two Peoples Bay Nature Reserve east of Albany, while looking for **Quokkas** on the mainland, a team rediscovered it by chance. Today it's considered the world's rarest marsupial and one of Australia's most endangered mammals. Using dense, grey-brown fur and a slender curved snout it tunnels through dense heath, digging for food. Like most Australian mammals of this small size, foxes and feral cats are driving this rare, shy marsupial to a possible early extinction. Native predators like carpet pythons also play their part, along with bushfires, but a new threat to these creatures, with their now very low population, is the loss of genetic diversity.

On the south-eastern Australian coast a similar story is playing out for the **Long-footed Potoroo**. Its range, extending from Gippsland in Victoria to just north of the border with New South Wales, is shrinking and fragmenting.

The **Long-footed Potoroos** grow to the size of a rabbit with very long hind feet. Their entire body length is 38-42cm - then add the tail. This potoroo hops like a kangaroo, can grasp objects with its tail and has soft dense fur, a grayish-brown that fades to a lighter underbelly.

The **Long-footed Potoroo** is a very shy and elusive nocturnal species. It was not studied until 1967, so is not well understood. Natural predators like **Powerful owls** hunt them in the grassy open forest, but they have no natural defenses to introduced species like foxes, wild dogs and feral cats. They can be plucked easily out of their above-ground burrows or nests, which are tunnelled into dense thicket and heathland or in large stands of coastal grasstree scrub.

Eastern Barred Bandicoot

The difference between a potoroo and a bandicoot is obvious when you startle them feeding at night. A potoroo hops or bounds like a small kangaroo and the bandicoot scuttles away like a rabbit.

The **Eastern Barred Bandicoot** weighs less than 2kg, has a short tail and three to four whitish bars across its grey-brindled fur rump. These bandicoots have two wild populations, one in Victoria and one on the island of Tasmania. The species is nocturnal, emerging from its burrow at dusk to dig for fungi, buried and growing on the roots of trees. It also forages for a variety of invertebrates including crickets, beetles and earthworms.

Due to foxes, cats and natural predators, bushfires and similar threats, the Victorian population of these bandicoots is struggling. Ongoing conservation endeavours such as captive breeding programmes, the use of fences to create predation free zones, repopulating areas with captive stocks and rewilding have all been attempted to ensure their survival.

Iconic Koala and an Island Echidna

Australia has always been considered a tinderbox. Often a sunburnt, drought ravaged country, it's been shaped by fire for tens of thousands of years, the first Australians using fire as part of a ritual regeneration of the forests. With age-old traditional burning they promoted the abundance of their resources, using fire to make easier hunting for food and to reduce the risk of wildfires. In recent times large bushfires have devastated local human and animal communities across the country. For seven long months in late 2019-2020, Australia saw almost unprecedented fires with up to 24 million hectares burnt: property, lives and bushland literally incinerated. An estimated 3 billion bush creatures were killed and countless thousands left injured. Many were rescued and rehabilitated, but many more were humanely put down. The bush and some animal species will recover, but these fires have put many bush creatures on the Endangered list, including two of our most endearing and iconic.

On the Australian mainland, urban development and expansion, including the construction of roads and highways, has reduced and fractured huge tracts of natural **Koala** habitat. **Koalas** have a specialised diet of very specific eucalyptus trees. Although in some areas they may seem robust and plentiful - and one of Australia's cutest tourist attractions - these sleepy marsupials are dependent on ever decreasing stands of eucalypts to survive. In the last few decades, disease and loss of habitat have reduced their overall numbers, but effective conservation efforts in some places have seen localised populations returned to healthy, sustainable levels. However, since the 2020 fires, the plight of these iconic **Koalas** is critical once again - some of the last healthy strongholds were reduced to cinders in the holocaust. It's not just critical in well-known pockets like Kangaroo Island or parts of the Otways, the **Koala** is now endangered across almost its entire range. Bushfires and natural disasters only go to highlight how important it is that we plan our future and manage our country better, for the health of our landscapes and our bush creatures, which we surely want to remain healthy, wild and free for many years to come.

These historic fires not only ravaged the mainland. On Kangaroo Island, near Adelaide, lightning strikes started a wildfire that eventually broke containment lines and burned though bushland, scarring 50% of the island. The fire killed wildlife, devastated the landscape, and reduced resources for the surviving native animals. In the wake of this firestorm, the native population of **Kangaroo Island Echidnas** dwindled to critical numbers. Early action and recovery programmes have been put in place, thanks to their listing as an Endangered species, so there is hope.

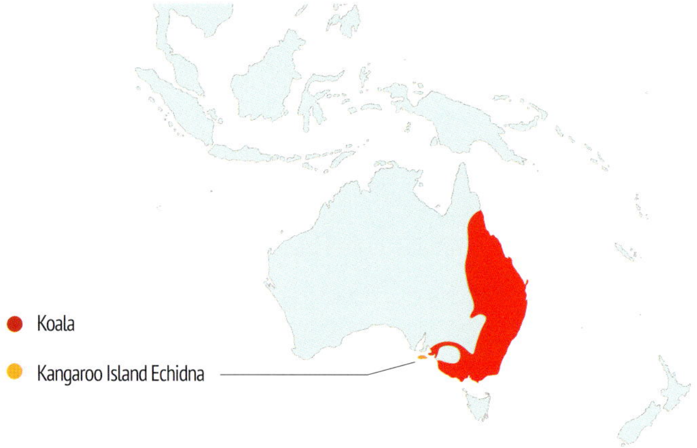

THIS PAGE
A Kangaroo Island Echidna on the hunt for ants.

OPPOSITE PAGE
A Koala struggles to survive in burnt out bushland, as the wind changes direction producing a second ember attack.

Australia's Elusive Endangered Marsupials

You'd be really lucky if you came across these marsupials in the wild. Hiding amongst the sun-kissed rocks and rusty coloured outcrops of central Western Australia is the shy and very agile Black-flanked Rock-wallaby. In its tree hollows, small dens and burrows in Arnhem Land, the small spotted cat-like Northern Quoll waits for the cover of night. In Gippsland Victoria, the larger and highly elusive Tiger Quoll prowls the cool evenings hunting rodents and nesting birds. In the south-west corner of Australia the timid banded anteater or Numbat hunts for ants with its long tongue. All these marsupials are some of our most Endangered bush creatures.

The **Black-flanked Rock-wallaby** is quite small, living amongst rocky outcrops and caves in only three isolated ranges of the western Kimberleys. It emerges at dusk to feed on grass, leaves, bark and fruits, but can sometimes be glimpsed during the day soaking up the sun. The rocky refuges are key to the wallaby's survival, affording it some protection from introduced predators like the fox. Unfortunately much of its habitat has been cleared for farming.

In the Jarrah forests of Western Australia lives a small banded anteater - the **Numbat**. They don't actually eat ants but their long sticky tongues are excellent for picking up termites, which they exclusively forage for. On a good day, they will eat 20,000 termites! Under threat from habitat loss, and easy prey for foxes and cats, they have been reduced to fewer than 1,000 individuals in the wild. The last remaining populations have so far survived these new predators because of a naturally occurring toxin found in the Poison Pea plant. The Pea contains sodium fluoroacetate, the active ingredient used in 1080 baits. **Numbats** have evolved alongside these plants and have a tolerance to the toxin. However, it's lethal to most introduced species.

The **Northern Quoll** is the smallest of the four nocturnal Quoll species. They maybe small, but they are the most aggressive of all the quolls. Communicating through hissing, these cat-like marsupials are also great tree climbers. Apart from predators, a major threat to the **Northern Quoll** is poisoning by eating introduced cane toads.

In comparison, the **Spotted Tiger Quoll** is the largest of the quolls. Also nocturnal, they hunt with an agile bounding gait and rest during the day in dens. Males can travel large distances seeking females, but this makes them easy prey for feral cats and foxes. Bushfires and cattle grazing have also impacted all these native marsupials, but they persist, holding out in isolated pockets of our remaining wilderness. They all need our help and mindful conservation or they are likely to continue down the road to an unnecessary extinction.

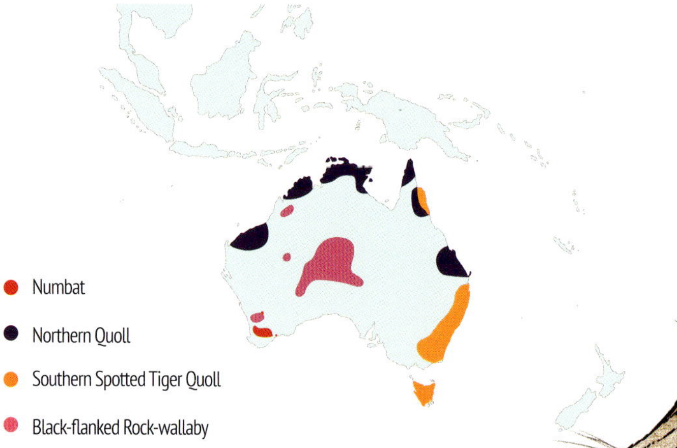

THIS SPREAD

Hiding in the high rocky outcrops are three Black-flanked Rock Wallabies, while on the Arnhem Land Plateau (bottom right) two brown Northern Quolls roam. The eastern bushland reveals a growling Tiger Quoll, and the dry scrubland of the west (left) camouflages a couple of striped Numbats.

THIS PAGE
Clockwise from top right; A Sydney Hawk Dragonfly perches on a vine; a couple of Vesk's Plant-louse hang out; three Tasmanian Torrent Midges; two Dinosaur Ants; a Bornemissza's stag beetle; a resting Golden Sun Moth; and two hiding Southern Sandstone Cave Crickets.

OPPOSITE PAGE
The Blue-banded Bee, is a symbol of native bee fragility.

Australia's Endangered Insects

Every bush creature exists as an answer to the riddle of survival. Every time we lose a species, we lose their interactions with other parts of their ecosystem - puzzle pieces that can be very important. In the case of insects, we may lose the specialised and critical services of pollination that they provide. Such relationships are often highly specific and so inter-dependent that the loss of one species has the potential to drag other species to extinction along with it.

Insects have evolved alongside plants for hundreds of millions of years. When the first flowers emerged, insects quickly began to work in perfect symbiosis with their new partners, pollinating and sometimes working as forest pest control. Insects are also major agents of the disposal of dead plants and animals, help create and maintain healthy soil and most breed in their millions, supplying a vital food source for a wide range of bats, other insects, birds and rodents. The diversity of the insect world, vast array of species and their adaptations to so many different niches is just mindboggling. Many insect species, however, are now under threat.

The **Tasmanian Torrent Midge** is not a nasty mosquito, it's a lanky-legged species of fly native to Australia. As the name suggests, they live in the moist splash-zones and micro-environments near fastest-flowing streams of north-eastern Tasmania. The fact that this midge is not found anywhere else makes it particularly vulnerable.

Then there is the **Vesk's Plant-louse** which was only discovered in 2007. It is the only species of plant-louse currently listed as Endangered in the world, mostly because of its very limited range. It was discovered in the bio-diverse Stirling Range National Park, in south-west Australia: a large bushfire could easily cause this plant louse's premature extinction.

In New South Wales, in a small area south of Sydney, habitat loss, irregular river flow, pollution and vegetation degradation have seen the population decline of the rare and distinctive **Sydney Hawk Dragonfly**. Now listed as an Endangered species, this predatory dragonfly has pretty specific habitat requirements that don't mix well with the urban, industrial and agricultural developments in their waterways.

The **Southern Sandstone Cave Cricket** is specific to a few sandstone caves, crevices and rock overhangs in the Bates Creek area. Also known as the **Francistown Cave Cricket**, it's been observed on semi-moist to dry walls, often grazing near lichen and mosses. The crickets emerge at night to feed in the forest. Very little else is known about them. Their main threats are nearby logging, caving and cave tourism.

Let's move out of these caves and into the sun-soaked grasslands of Wangaratta, in north-east Victoria. There we find a unique ornate moth called the **Golden Sun Moth** that inhabits the scrub. With clubbed antennae, a notable feature as most moths have brushy antennae, the **Golden Sun Moth** prefers a particular species of grass giving it a very limited range - and thus susceptible to extinction.

Bornemissza's Stag Beetle belongs to a group of flightless, black, ground-dwelling beetles. It is found in only five small locations in the mature wet or damp eucalypt forests endemic to north-eastern Tasmania. Forestry practices pose the greatest threat to **Bornemissza's Stag Beetle**, given that much of its habitat is in state managed land. Wildfire is a serious threat and has the potential to wipe this beetle off the map. Firewood collection also occurs at all five sites, often removing the moist woody habitat these beetles need to survive.

A relative of the bull ant, the **Dinosaur Ant** is considered one of the closest species, biologically speaking, to the earliest ants. Known as 'living fossils', they offer valuable insights into ant evolution and have a wasp-like appearance (ants evolved from wasps over 100 million years ago). The **Dinosaur Ant** forages, individually, from dusk until dawn in eucalyptus trees, preying on other insects. Bushfires are a major threat to these ants due to their dependence on fire-prone eucalyptus trees.

Finally, the devastating 2019–2020 bushfires had a significant impact on our native Australian bees. Of the 553 Australian native bee species discovered, 11 are now listed as Threatened. Prior to the fires, only three bee species were listed as Threatened. The Blue-banded Bee isn't endangered, but the very specific role they play as 'buzz pollinators' leaves their fate at risk too. It might well become endangered with the increasing threat of bushfires and climate change.

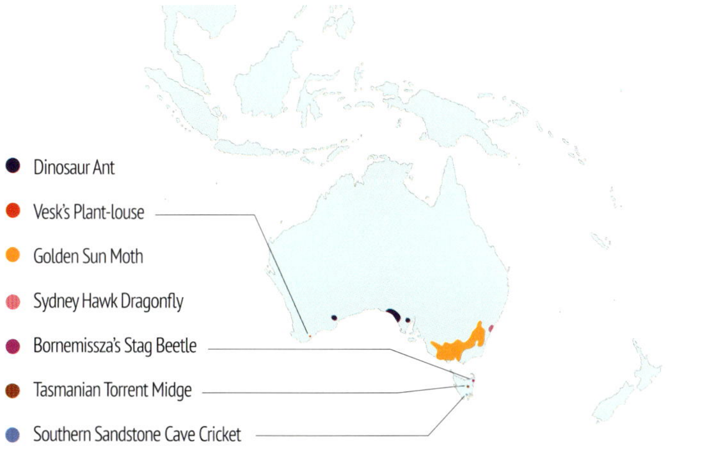

The Lord Howe Island Stick Insect or Phasmid

The 'Tree Lobster', a phasmid most commonly known as the Lord Howe Island Stick Insect, was thought to be extinct by 1920 after black rats infested the island. However, in 1964, a team of climbers visiting the rocky islet or sea stack called Ball's Pyramid, 23 kilometres south-east of Lord Howe, discovered the dead remains of one of these creatures. Over the years, more remains were collected: the species was living there! No expedition was successful, however, in finding a live specimen. Then amazingly, in 2001, an Australian scientist and a Park Ranger climbed 100 metres up the pyramid after dark to discover a lone colony of 24 Lord Howe Island Stick Insects in a crevice. Celebrated as "the rarest insect in the world", the rediscovery sparked a now world famous recovery and captive breeding programme that should see these bush creatures return to their wild and natural habitat on Lord Howe Island.

The **Lord Howe Island Stick Insect** is a fascinating bush creature with a grand story of survival. Since 2001, the Melbourne Zoo has successfully bred and recovered the species, and plans to re-establish it back on Lord Howe island. To ensure these phasmids survive, Melbourne Zoo has also sent eggs to the Bristol Zoo in England, the San Diego Zoo in the United States and the Toronto Zoo in Canada. So now four zoos are taking part in the ongoing effort to recover and de-list this rare and Critically Endangered stick insect.

Because the **Lord Howe Island Stick Insect** had been so elusive, little was known about this phasmid other than some sketchy historical records. Even finding it on Ball's Pyramid, after 35 years of 'extinction', offered only small clues to its breeding, diet and other natural behaviours.

Everything that is known about this species is highly unusual compared to its mainland stick insect counterparts. Firstly, they are flightless - creatures on small islands with airborne predecessors often are. The males and females form a bond in some pairs. The females lay eggs while hanging from branches. and hatching takes place nine months later. The nymphs emerge bright green and are really quite active during the day. Yet as they mature, they turn jet black and become nocturnal. Finally, without the presence of males the females can resort to parthenogenesis: producing viable eggs - and thus young - without mating.

Nature always seems to surprise us: often discoveries are waiting just around the corner or under the next rock we turn over. That's just one exciting thing about studying ecology and the natural world. In 2014 a team of unauthorised climbers scaled the summit of Ball's Pyramid. They sighted another colony of these amazing creatures 500ms up, clinging to vegetation growing from a small crevice and soil trapped in cracks at the summit. It's hard to believe how they have survived in the wild for so long when you consider the terrain, the location, the weather, the ocean: basically their extreme toehold on survival. This is the ultimate cliff-hanger of a survival story!

Appearance *As a nymph the Lord Howe Island Stick Insect starts out bright green and well camouflaged, but as they mature their strange oblong shape turns black. Males are quite a bit smaller than the females, with thicker thighs and sturdy legs. Unlike most other stick insects, they have no wings.* **Size** *An adult Lord Howe Island Stick Insect can measure up to 20cm in length and weigh in at around 25g, while the females are 25% larger.*

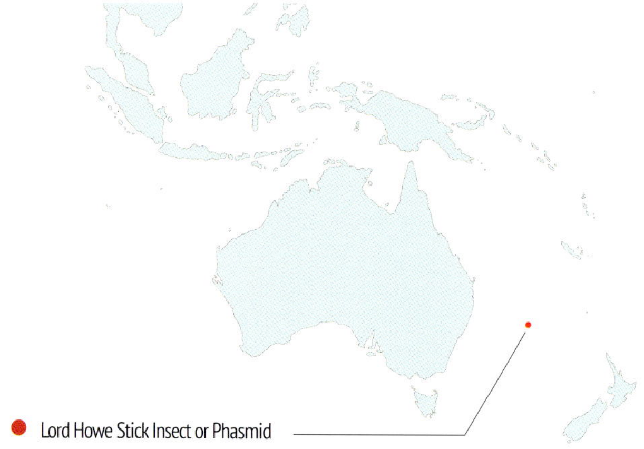

OPPOSITE PAGE
With Lord Howe Island visible in the distance, a Lord Howe Island Stick Insect clings to the vertical walls of Ball's Pyramid, surviving against the odds on this isolated outcrop.

Australia's Diminishing Land Snails

It is thought that land snails worldwide are threatened with, proportionally, the "greatest number of extinctions". More than birds, more than mammals, more than reptiles or even frogs, snails are on a slippery slope. Today in Australia our native land snails are really vulnerable to any eco-disturbance: poisons, habitat loss and especially the threat of introduced predators. That at least a dozen species of endemic snails are listed as Critically Endangered, yet are rarely discussed in school classrooms, is cause for concern. They truly need all the love, support and attention they can get right now.

Predation has been a big theme within these pages. Invasive species, whether introduced by accident or purposefully, upset the balance of any ecology. Australian environments have evolved over many millennia and, if disturbed, it takes more millennia to find balance again. Along the way native flora and fauna can be pushed to extinction. Most of our endangered land snails are tiny and endemic to remote islands such as Lord Howe Island, Norfolk Island and small Phillip Island.

The main reason many of these snails have gone extinct or are now critically endangered is because of invasive rats accidently transported to the islands by trade ships. Bird species like the **Lord Howe Fantail**, **Robust White-eye**, and **Island Thrush** were all wiped out by black rats that arrived in 1918. After the food source of eggs and chicks disappeared, the island's snails became the next delicious survival snack.

Rat eradication started in the 1920s with large introduced Masked and Barn Owls, but the bigger owls saw the smaller **Lord Howe Boobook** (Morepork) die out. A new 2019 rodent eradication programme was considered complete in 2021, with 210,000 rats removed, so hopefully we will see a re-emergence of these land snails, with many of these species bouncing back.

On the Australian mainland a similar story plays out. The **Mitchell's Rainforest Snail's** shell measures up to 4.5cm across and is reddish brown to black with distinct yellow banding, while its soft parts are black. This nocturnal snail feeds upon leaf litter, fungi and lichen, and it used to be commonly found in rainforests and swampy parts of the northern coastal lowlands of New South Wales. Apart from introduced rats and birds, the **Mitchell's Rainforest Snail's** major threats consist of herbicides, pesticides, fires, weed invasion and local deforestation.

The **Rosewood Keeled Snail** of Western Australia and the Northern Territory grows to around 1.4cm and lives among scattered limestone boulders in open savannah areas subject to flooding. These snails climb trees to survive floods, but cane toads, cattle grazing and changing vegetation structure caused by weed invasion is slowly having an impact - resulting in its inclusion on the Critically Endangered list.

The **Boggonmoss Snail/Dawson Valley Snail** of Queensland grows a 2.5cm shell and is grey with a mustard coloured mantle and distinct irregular black blotches. It faces a triple threat of predation, with cane toads, mice and rats all killing off populations.

While the mainland has less endangered land snails, Lord Howe Island harbours Australia's highest diversity of land snails, with an estimated 65-70 endemic species. Five of these species have declined so drastically that they are considered Endangered or Critically Endangered, and some are feared extinct. Recent surveys have rediscovered one species on Norfolk Island and neighbouring Phillip Island has an important role to play in the preservation of these remote island land snails.

In May 2021, scientists from the Australian Museum Research Institute, working with the Taronga Zoo, collected some live land snails from the three Tasman Sea islands to start a captive breeding programme. Even after the team surveyed the islands, it's been hard to determine whether several species should be recorded as extinct. Between the islands, 10 land snails are now listed as Endangered or Critically Endangered and five more not listed here are already presumed extinct. That extinction rate is alarmingly high.

On Lord Howe Island the Endangered species are: the **Magnificent Helicarionid Land Snail**, **Mount Lidgebird Charopid Land Snail**, **Lord Howe Flax Snail**, **Masters' Charopid Land Snail** and **Whitelegge's Land Snail**.
On Norfolk and Phillip Islands combined the list comprises: **Campbell's Helicarionid Land Snail**, **Gray's Helicarionid Land Snail**, **Phillip Island Helicarionid Land Snail** and **Stoddart's Helicarionid Land Snail** and **Suter's Helicarionid Land Snail**.

We are often taught to think of snails as pests and not good for our gardens, but they are a vital part of our ecosystems, be they forests, savannahs or islands. These precious bush creatures can be easily overlooked when it comes to our limited understanding of the natural world, but they are an important part of the food chain and have existed for hundreds of millions of years.

THIS SPREAD
1. Mitchell's Rainforest Snail, 2. Rosewood keeled Snail, 3. Boggonmoss Snail/Dawson Valley Snail, 4. Campbell's Helicarionid Land Snail, 5. Gray's Helicarionid Land Snail, 6. Lord Howe flax Snail, 7. Phillip Island Helicarionid Land Snail, 8. Masters' Charopid Land Snail, 9. Mount Lidgebird Charopid Land Snail, 10. Whitelegge's Land Snail, 11. Stoddart's Helicarionid Land Snail, 12. Magnificent Helicarionid Land Snail, 13. Suter's Helicarionid Land Snail.

Purple-crowned Fairy-wren

The greatest threat to this bush creature is its loss of habitat. Livestock and feral water buffalo, seeking water, trample their riparian vegetation, specifically pandanus. More recently, intense bushfires have seen a 41% decline in their populations.

The distinctive **Purple-crowned Fairy-wren** is one of the larger fairy-wrens. There are two subspecies: the western subspecies is exclusive to the Northern Territory, while the eastern subspecies' range extends into north-western Queensland. Conservation research and efforts for recovery are underway on Mornington Island. Due to their exclusively favouring pandanus palms for nesting sites, they are almost entirely restricted to a narrow band along well-vegetated river channels.

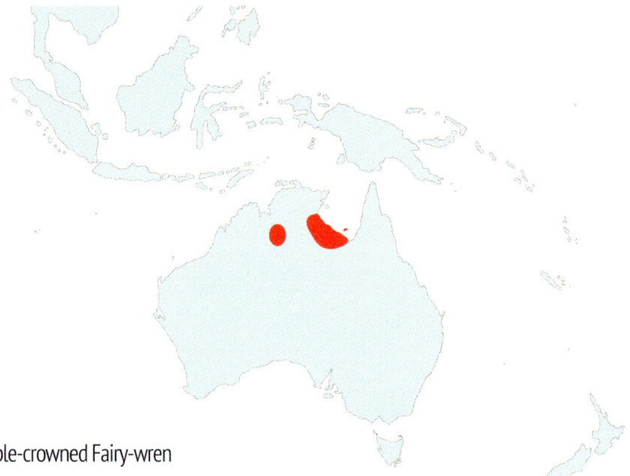

A catalogue record for this book is available from the National Library of Australia

MIX
Paper from responsible sources
FSC® C023121

Woodslane Press Pty Ltd
10 Apollo Street
Warriewood, NSW 2102
Email: info@woodslane.com.au
Tel: 02 8445 2300
Website: www.woodslanepress.com.au

Published in Australia in 2022 by Woodslane Press

Printed in China by Hang Tai
Designed by Myke Mollard
Special thanks to Dennis Jones, James Beckingham and Yiwen Yao for all the enthusiasm and support in making this dream happen.

THIS PAGE
Purple-Crowned Fairy-wren.

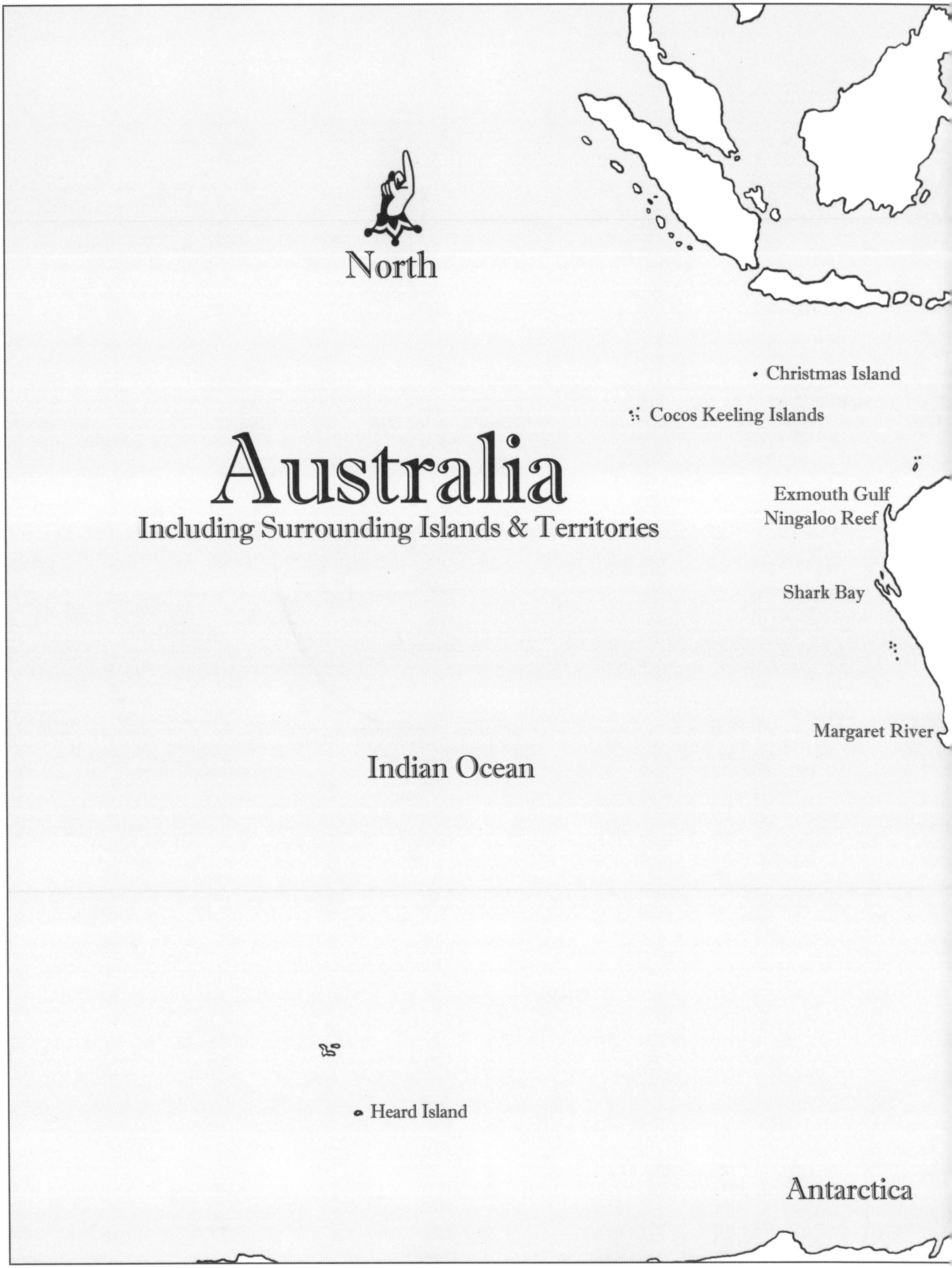
North
Christmas Island
Cocos Keeling Islands
Australia
Including Surrounding Islands & Territories
Exmouth Gulf
Ningaloo Reef
Shark Bay
Margaret River
Indian Ocean
Heard Island
Antarctica